O V I D
METAMORPHOSES
BOOK I

OVID
METAMORPHOSES
BOOK I

Edited by

A.G. Lee

Published by
BRISTOL CLASSICAL PRESS (U.K.)
General Editor: John H. Betts
and
BOLCHAZY-CARDUCCI PUBLISHERS (U.S.A.)
(by arrangement with the
Syndicate of the Cambridge University Press)

Cover illustration: Apollo and Daphne, after the
sculpture by Bernini, *Galleria Borghese,* Rome.
(Drawing by Marion Perry.)

Printed in the United States of America

First published by Cambridge University Press, 1953
and reprinted up to 1979 by them.

Reprinted, with permission of the Syndicate of the
Cambridge University Press, 1984 & 1988 by

U.K.	U.S.A.
BRISTOL CLASSICAL PRESS	**BOLCHAZY-CARDUCCI**
226 North Street	**PUBLISHERS**
Bedminster	1000 Brown Street, Unit 101
Bristol BS3 1JD	Wauconda, IL 60084
ISBN 0-86292-144-9	ISBN 0-86516-040-6

CONTENTS

PREFACE

This edition is intended for Sixth Forms and Undergraduates, though parts of it may possibly be of interest to professional scholars. I have tried to improve upon the edition of L. D. Dowdall published by the Cambridge University Press in 1892. Much work has been done on Ovid since that time and I hope that some of its results may be apparent in the following pages.

The Text is based on that of Hugo Magnus (Berlin, 1914). Those who are interested in such matters can find in the Critical Notes a discussion of those places (some thirty in number, and excluding variations in orthography) in which I differ from him.

In writing the Explanatory Notes I have referred to many earlier editors, in particular to Burman and Lemaire, but above all to Haupt-Ehwald. Deferrari's *Concordance of Ovid* has of course proved invaluable. I have also to thank Mr B. Goulding Brown for kindly allowing me to consult on several points his notes of Housman's lectures on this book.

In writing the Introduction I have chiefly consulted the work of S. G. Owen, A. L. Wheeler, Edgar Martini, Hermann Fränkel, and Walther Kraus.

I am deeply indebted to Professor R. J. Getty, my former teacher, and to Professor R. A. B. Mynors for many valuable suggestions and for pointing out a number of mistakes; those that remain are my own responsibility. I also wish to thank all others who have helped me in various ways, but especially

Mr H. H. Huxley for sharing the work of proof-reading and for suggesting several improvements.

A. G. LEE

St John's College

INTRODUCTION

A. OVID'S LIFE AND CHARACTER

The best account of Ovid's life is the poet's own autobiography, composed in exile for the benefit of posterity. It is the beautiful tenth poem in the fourth book of the *Tristia*, written with a simplicity and restraint that cannot fail to win the reader's interest and sympathy. The details given there can be supplemented from other passages in Ovid's own works and in those of the elder Seneca.[1]

Publius Ovidius Naso was a Paelignian, born at Sulmo (the modern Sulmona), a *municipium* some ninety miles east of Rome, on 20 March 43 B.C. Just over a year before, Caesar had been murdered, and in the following December Cicero was to be assassinated to satisfy the hatred of Antony. Ovid came of an old equestrian family. Inscriptions show that the name Ovidius was a common one in the district of Sulmo. He was proud of his descent, proud too of the part played by his countrymen in their fight for liberty in the Social War (*Am.* 3, 15, 9-10), and proud of his birthplace with its fertile vineyards and well watered fields (*Am.* 2, 16, 1 ff.). At an early age he was sent with his brother, who was exactly one year older than himself, to Rome to be educated by the best teachers, for their father was ambitious for his sons' career. Ovid was quick to display an interest in poetry and to try his hand at writing verses of his own. Like Pope,

---

[1] For statements supported by *Tr.* 4, 10, I have not as a rule quoted reff.

he 'lisp'd in numbers, for the numbers came'.[1] But his father did not approve of such an unprofitable pursuit, arguing that even Homer died in poverty. There is a story in one of the late *Lives* of the poet, which, though probably apocryphal, is amusingly apt. According to this, when Ovid was once being beaten by his father for spending so much time on his verses, the young poet begged for mercy in the extempore line 'parce mihi, numquam uersificabo, pater'!

After his days with the *grammaticus*, about which we have no information, Ovid proceeded to the schools of rhetoric, where he was a pupil of Porcius Latro, a Spaniard from Corduba, and of Arellius Fuscus, who was probably by birth a Greek of Asia Minor; both men were among the foremost rhetoricians of their day. The elder Seneca, a friend of Latro, has added to our knowledge of Ovid at this period of his life. He tells us that Ovid was regarded as a good declaimer; that his style was just like verse in a prose dress; and that he admired Latro enough to bring many of his epigrams into his own poetry. Seneca adds that Ovid seldom declaimed *controuersiae*, and then only when they turned on a moral point ('declamabat . . . Naso raro controuersias et non nisi ethicas'); he preferred to deliver *suasoriae* (Sen. *Contr.* 2, 2, 8-12). This is an interesting point which for full understanding requires a knowledge of the difference between the two rhetorical exercises—*controuersia* and *suasoria*.

The *controuersia* was an exercise in the judicial branch of oratory; it was in fact a fictitious lawsuit. The facts were given and could not be disputed; it was the pupil's task to interpret them and practise

[1] Cf. *Tr.* 4, 10, 26: 'et quod temptabam dicere uersus erat', and Pope *Ep. to Dr. Arbuthnot* 1. 128.

himself either in prosecution or in defence. Seneca has recorded part of a speech made by Ovid in a *controuersia* which he himself heard. This will serve as a good example of the type. The imaginary facts of the case are these: a husband and wife swear an oath that if one of them dies the other will commit suicide. The husband then sets out on a journey and sends a message to his wife announcing his death. His wife, true to her promise, attempts to kill herself, but fails in her purpose and is later restored to health. At this juncture her father steps into the story. He orders her, with all the moral authority of a Roman father, to divorce her husband. She refuses. Her father disinherits her. The husband is then supposed to bring an action against the father. It fell to Ovid on this occasion to take the husband's side. It is to be noted that the story on which the *controuersia* is based is extremely unlikely, but that is a general characteristic of the type. A fantastic theme gave more scope for imagination and ingenuity of argument. It will be seen too that this particular *controuersia* is an 'ethical' one; that is to say, it turns on a moral point and affords scope for the delineation of character. As Seneca has told us, this was the only form of *controuersia* in which Ovid took part. He disliked the logical presentation of arguments (*argumentatio*), preferring the appeal to the emotions, as one might expect of a poet.

The *suasoria* was an exercise in the deliberative branch of oratory. Unlike the *controuersia* it had reference to the future, and was concerned with advising the right course of action in a particular set of circumstances. The subjects were usually chosen from history or legend. For example, Agamemnon is ordered to sacrifice Iphigenia; his advisers come forward and give their reasons why he should or should not obey. Ovid probably preferred this exercise because the pleader had a freer hand than in the *controuersia*; it was more dramatic and demanded greater psychological insight. The results of this training can be seen in the great monologues of the *Metamorphoses* (see 618 n.), as when Medea debates whether to help Jason or not, and particularly in the famous debate (in *Met.* 13) between Ajax and Ulysses over the arms of Achilles.

It was, then, by such exercises as these that Ovid's wits were sharpened and his powers of expression developed in the rhetorical schools. It was probably after completing his studies here that, at about the age of nineteen, he went to Athens with the object of finishing his education.[1] There, if we may judge from the report of his own course of studies that the younger Cicero sent home to his father, Ovid would continue the practice of declamation and devote a good deal of time to the study of philosophy. We do not know how long he stayed in Athens. Perhaps it was at the end of his time there that he went on with his friend, the poet Macer, to visit the cities of Asia Minor.[2] We may guess that together they made the same kind of tour as did Horace's friend Bullatius (see Hor. *Epist.* 1, 11). Ovid himself tells us that he visited the site of Troy and was there shown the spot where the Palladium, the famous image of Pallas, had fallen down from heaven (*Fasti* 6, 421-4). In the company of this same friend he travelled to Sicily and saw Etna, Henna and Syracuse (*Ex P.* 2, 10, 22 ff.). This is all the information

[1] *Tr.* 1, 2, 77: 'petii studiosus Athenas'.
[2] *Ex P.* 2, 10, 21. This was certainly not Aemilius Macer of Verona, who was an older man than Ovid (see p. 17). It may have been the Pompeius Macer mentioned in Suet. *Jul.* 56 as Augustus' librarian.

we have about the poet's travels, except that much
later, in A.D. 8, when he received news of his banish-
ment, he was on the island of Elba in the company of
his powerful friend Cotta Maximus (*Ex P.* 2, 3, 83-4).

When Ovid's education was ended, he took the first
steps towards a political career by holding certain
minor administrative offices. He became one of the
tresuiri capitales, or police magistrates. He was also
one of the *centumuiri*, a panel of judges whose main
business was to deal with testamentary cases, and he
mentions having acted as a single judge in private
lawsuits (*Tr.* 2, 93-6, *Ex P.* 3, 5, 23-4). These minor
posts would normally have led to the quaestorship,
which as the lowest office in the *cursus honorum* gave
its holder a seat in the Senate. But at this stage in his
life Ovid decided to abandon a political career and
devote himself to the pursuit of poetry.

He had begun to give public recitations of his poems
at an early age (see *Tr.* 4, 10, 57-8), and it was not long
before he acquired wide popularity as a poet of love.
His individual works will be described later in this
introduction. Suffice it to say here that his total out-
put, as we have received it, exceeds that of Lucretius,
Catullus, Virgil, Horace and Tibullus put together; it
amounts to some 33,000 lines, the equivalent of about
three and a half *Aeneids*. Its popularity among his
contemporaries is attested by his own words 'in toto
plurimus orbe legor' (*Tr.* 4, 10, 128; see also *Tr.* 2,
115-20 and 5, 7, 25-8), and by the quotations from his
poetry scrawled on walls in Pompeii.[1]

---

[1] E.g. 'quid pote tan durum saxso aut quid mollius unda? /
dura tamen molli saxsa cauantur aqua'; a misquotation, as far
as the first line is concerned, of *A.A.* 1, 475-6: 'quid magis est
saxo durum, quid mollius unda?' etc.

Ovid was married three times, but he does not tell us the name of any of his wives. He describes the first as 'nec digna nec utilis'; he was married to her when he was little more than a boy, and the marriage did not last long. His second wife was blameless ('sine crimine'), but again the marriage was cut short, perhaps by her death. It was probably this second wife who was the mother of Ovid's only daughter, already a married woman at the time of his banishment (see *Tr.* 1, 3, 19 and *Fasti* 6, 219 ff.). His third wife was connected with the powerful family of the Fabii, being a companion of Marcia, the wife of Fabius Maximus (*Ex P.* 1, 2, 136). Ovid lived happily with her for many years and shows his affection for her in several of the letters in verse written during his banishment.

Ovid knew most of the poets of his day. Though he had only seen Virgil, he had heard Horace giving a reading from his *Odes*, and had been introduced to Tibullus. He was an intimate friend of Propertius and of other poets who are mere names to us now, such as Ponticus and Bassus. As regards his relations with the Roman nobility, Ovid tells us that it was Messalla, the patron of Tibullus, who first urged him to publish his poetry (*Ex P.* 2, 3, 77-8). He was probably one of his *clientes*, for he reminds Messalla's elder son Messallinus of how he had written a funeral ode for his father (*Ex P.* 1, 7, 27-30), and writes to the younger son, Cotta Maximus, asserting that he first knew him as a baby in arms (*Ex P.* 2, 3, 71-2). Ovid also had some connexion with Sextus Pompey, descendant of an uncle of Pompey the Great. He addresses four letters to him (*Ex P.* 4, 1, 4, 5 and 15), testifies to generous financial help and thanks him for safeguarding his journey into exile. Finally, Ovid also had the patronage of Fabius Maximus, whose wedding song he had composed and whose hospitality he often enjoyed (*Ex P.* 1, 2, 129 ff.). As for the Imperial house, Ovid had no direct connexions there, except that his third wife was a protégée of the younger Atia, who was aunt of Augustus and mother of Fabius' wife, Marcia. From all this it is clear that Ovid, before his banishment, must have been a well-known figure in literary circles at Rome and had access to influential Romans of the highest rank in society.

But these connexions availed him little when misfortune overtook him. In A.D. 8, at the age of fifty, he was commanded by the Emperor to leave Italy and go into banishment at Tomi (the modern Constanza in Rumania) on the shores of the Black Sea.[1] The cause of this harsh decree is obscure and all the efforts of scholars to discover it have so far proved inconclusive. Ovid himself tells us that there were two causes—'a poem and a mistake' (*Tr.* 2, 207 'carmen et error'). The poem was his *Ars Amatoria,* which had first appeared as long ago as A.D.1. Its spirit was directly contrary to Augustus' policy of encouraging marriage and a stable family life based on the old Roman domestic virtues. But the immediate cause must have been the 'mistake', and this Ovid does not explain. He hints at it merely, for apparently his readers knew all about it (*Tr.* 4, 10, 99). From his veiled references we can only gather the following general facts: he had accidentally witnessed some crime (*Tr.* 3, 5, 49-50); this was closely concerned with

[1] The correct Latin form is *Tomis.* I have retained Tomi as sanctioned by usage. In the same way it is customary to write *Virgil,* not *Vergil,* in English.

Augustus (*Tr.* 2, 133-4); fear made him keep his mouth shut, though if he had confided in a friend he would have been safe (*Ex P.* 2, 2, 17, *Tr.* 3, 6, 11); he had committed no illegal action (*Ex P.* 2, 9, 71). Unfortunately these indications are too vague to enable us to determine precisely what it was that Ovid had seen. It should be noted that he was not exiled in the technical sense—he was relegated, and therefore retained his civic rights and his property and was allowed to correspond freely with friends in Rome. But his case was unique in that he was sent to so remote and inhospitable a spot as Tomi. As a rule even exiles, in the strict sense, were permitted to remain in the Mediterranean area. It is evident that Augustus for reasons of his own wished to have Ovid as far away from Rome as possible, and with deliberate malice chose a place where the poet would be deprived of all the culture and refinement by which he set such store.

Of the hypotheses advanced as the cause of Ovid's banishment two have some plausibility. According to the first, which was elaborated, though not originated, by Boissier[1], Ovid was caught up in the intrigue of Decimus Silanus with the Emperor's granddaughter Julia, who was married to L. Aemilius Paullus. This supposition is given colour by the fact that Julia was apparently exiled in the same year as Ovid;[2] there is too the further point that the inclusion of the *Ars* in the count against Ovid suggests that his 'mistake' too was in some way connected with an offence against morality. To explain why his punishment took place so long after the publication of that work it is urged that Augustus had long been waiting for an opportunity to

---

[1] *L'opposition sous les Césars*, Paris, 1875, pp. 145 ff.
[2] Tac. *Ann.* 4, 71.

vent his displeasure on the author of a book so opposed
to the spirit of his whole social policy, and that Ovid's
mistake provided him with precisely the pretext for
which he had been looking.

According to the second theory, Ovid was accident-
ally involved in a plot to secure the succession for
Agrippa Postumus on the death of Augustus. This
Agrippa was the son of the Emperor's daughter Julia,
and was adopted by him at the same time as Tiberius.
He was exiled in A.D. 7, according to Tacitus, at the
instigation of Livia, who was anxious to secure her
own son's succession. The supporters of this theory lay
great stress on a passage in Tacitus (*Ann.* 1, 5).
Tacitus there records the existence of a rumour that
Augustus, shortly before his death, in the company of
Fabius Maximus (who, as we have already seen, was
Ovid's patron) visited his grandson Agrippa Postumus
on the island of Planasia. As a result of this meeting it
was hoped that Agrippa would be recalled from exile
and nominated Augustus' successor. Fabius entrusted
the secret to his wife Marcia, who thereupon informed
Livia; and very shortly afterwards Fabius died—
some thought by his own hand. Now Ovid, writing to
a friend about Fabius' death (*Ex P.* 4, 6, 9-16),
mentions that Fabius had resolved to appeal to
Augustus on his behalf and accuses himself of being
the cause of Fabius' fate. It has therefore been argued
that Ovid was in some way implicated in the affair of
Agrippa Postumus. As a further point in support of
this conjecture, it has been urged that on the death of
Augustus in A.D. 14, soon after that of Fabius, Ovid
seems at last to have abandoned all hope of recall from
banishment; for, so the argument continues, Tiberius
would naturally be unkindly disposed towards one

who had taken any part with his rival Agrippa. Indeed one of the first acts of Tiberius on assuming the purple was to put Agrippa to death.[1]

This theory is based on a series of supposed probabilities which in their turn are founded on a rumour; it is much less convincing than the first. The truth is that we do not know why Ovid was exiled and unless fresh evidence comes to light we are never likely to know. But though a mystery, the question will not cease to tempt the ingenuity of scholars.[2] Whatever the reason, Ovid left Italy in the early winter of A.D. 8 and arrived in Tomi during the following spring. He remained there, a broken man, until his death in A.D. 18.

Ovid must have been a fascinating character. The elder Seneca tells us that 'he had a refined, attractive and lovable disposition' ('habebat ille comptum et decens et amabile ingenium'—*Contr.* 2, 2, 8). To judge from his correspondence in exile he was a man with many friends. Men of sterner character than he, Lucretius perhaps, or Virgil, placed in his position

---

[1] This second theory is supported by S. Reinach (*Revue de Philologie* 34, 1910, pp. 345 ff.) and G. Némethy in the Excursus to his commentary on the *Tristia* and on the *Epistles from Pontus*. In the latter he is delighted to find that the initial letters of eight lines in *Ex P.* 4, 6, spell the name POSTUMUS, though the lines are neither consecutive nor systematically spaced. This aberration on the part of a scholar is rather amusing than convincing.—The present Poet Laureate in a good poem about Ovid called *A Letter from Pontus* has given an imaginary version of the events leading to his exile, combining both hypotheses.

[2] An interesting review of the problem by L. Herrmann, 'La Faute Secrète d'Ovide,' *Revue Belge de Philologie* 17(2), 1938, pp. 695 ff. He himself argues for the theory that Ovid violated the nocturnal rites of the Bona Dea when they were celebrated under the presidency of Livia in A.D. 8. But here again the evidence is insufficient.

might have drawn some consolation from philosophy during the long and weary years of banishment— would not at all events have given way under the burden of adversity as Ovid sometimes appears to have done. But if Tomi proves that Ovid was not a Cato, it proves too the acuteness of his sensibility to external impressions and the extent to which he was in love with the amenities and the elegances of life in the Mediterranean world as he knew it. His best poetry sprang from enjoyment and a sense of well-being, from a mind at ease. 'The fine-spun thread of poetry,' he writes, 'derives from serenity of mind' (*Tr.* 1, 1, 39); and again, 'Poetry is a labour of joy and demands a mind at peace' (*Tr.* 5, 12, 3-4). This mental poise was characteristic of the poet in the days before his banishment (*Ex P.* 4, 9, 91-2); it did not desert him altogether at Tomi, but the sense of joy had gone. One would guess that in his element he could be gay and witty and a brilliant conversationalist. He was a great lover of books and used them as a source of inspiration; he complains of his scanty library at Tomi (*Tr.* 3, 14, 37-8). But it would be as wrong to regard him as a bookish man as it would be to think of him as a social butterfly. Much as he loved Rome and its society, he loved the country too, and the landscape sketches here and there in his poetry show that he had a feeling for the beauty of natural scenery. He was himself something of a gardener, had planted apple-trees in the grounds of his villa near Rome and laments the fact that he cannot work on the land at Tomi (*Ex P.* 1, 8, 41 ff. and 4, 2, 43-4). He records his habit of composing poetry while reclining on a couch in his garden (*Tr.* 1, 11, 37; cf. *Tr.* 4, 8, 27). A leisured life was his choice, not for the sake of self-indulgence, but that he might devote himself to his art. He was abstemious in food and drink. He rarely drank wine, an unusual characteristic in a Roman (*Ex P.* 1, 10, 29 ff., 4, 2, 41). He had no taste for such amusements as gaming 'which waste that valuable thing—our time' (*Tr.* 2, 484).

The elder Seneca tells us two stories which illustrate Ovid's attitude towards the art for which he lived. On one occasion some friends of the poet's asked his permission to choose three lines from his works which they thought should be rejected. Ovid agreed on condition that he himself should choose three lines which he would not under any circumstances erase. When the two sides compared notes it was found that both had hit upon the same three lines.[1] Seneca concludes from this episode that Ovid did not 'lack judgement to correct the licence of his poetry, he lacked the inclination', and goes on to quote as a saying of the poet's that 'a face is the more attractive for having a mole on it'—'decentiorem faciem esse in qua aliquis naeuus fuisset' (*Contr.* 2, 2, 12). In the second story Ovid himself is seen as a critic. Varro of Atax, who translated the *Argonautica* of Apollonius Rhodius, had written the following lines (= Ap. Rhod. *Arg.* 3, 749-50):

'desierant latrare canes, urbesque silebant;
omnia noctis erant placida composta quiete.'

Ovid used to say of these verses that the second would be much improved if the sense ended after *erant*. He

---

[1] One was 'et gelidum Borean egelidumque Notum' (*Am.* 2, 11, 10), the second 'semibouemque uirum semiuirumque bouem' (*A.A.* 2, 24), the third we do not know owing to a lacuna in Seneca's text.

found, as Seneca points out, his own meaning in the line and that meaning was different from Varro's (*Contr.* 7, 1, 28). The suggested alteration is interesting because it shows, first, Ovid's power of seeing things in an individual way, and secondly, his leaning towards terse and pithy statement in verse.

But the keynote of his character is refinement. This idea is present in Seneca's description of his *comptum ingenium*. It is present too in Ovid's own explanation of his liking for the Augustan age in which he lived (*A.A.* 3, 121-8):

> 'prisca iuuent alios; ego me nunc denique natum
>   gratulor; haec aetas moribus apta meis:
> non quia nunc terrae lentum subducitur aurum,
>   lectaque diuerso litore concha uenit;
> nec quia decrescunt effosso marmore montes,
>   nec quia caeruleae mole fugantur aquae;
> sed quia cultus adest, nec nostros mansit in annos
>   rusticitas, priscis illa superstes auis.'

It was not wealth nor the material achievements of the time that appealed to him, but rather its culture, its refinement. And refinement again is the hall-mark of his own poetry. It would be hard to better the praise of Nicolaus Heinsius, greatest of Ovid's editors, when he writes that in Ovid's verse 'the weight and strength of Latin speech and the charm and elegance of Greece rival one another.'[1]

---

[1]   'in quibus eloquii pondus roburque Latini
              certat et Actaeo blandus ab orbe lepor.'
Lines 7 and 8 of the dedicatory poem in his edition of Ovid, published in 1661. The poem is printed in vol. 4 of Burman's Ovid, p. 164.

B. THE *METAMORPHOSES*

Ovid composed the *Metamorphoses* some time between
A.D. 2 and 8. He tells us that when sentence of
banishment was passed on him, the poem had not yet
been revised and lacked the last touches of the file—
'defuit et scriptis ultima lima meis' (*Tr.* 1, 7, 30). He
also states that in a fit of depression just before his
departure for Tomi he burnt his own copy of the poem.
Some scholars regard this merely as a theatrical
gesture on Ovid's part; he was anxious, so it is
argued, to rival Virgil, who left instructions that his
unfinished *Aeneid* should be destroyed by fire. But it
seems truer to human nature, and to the Italian
temperament, to suppose that in the utter despondency
caused by the news of his banishment Ovid for a time
lost his sense of proportion. However that may be,
various friends possessed copies of the work, and in
the early months of his exile Ovid sent home instruc-
tions for its publication and for the inclusion of the
following lines as an author's preface in apology for
its imperfections:

'orba parente suo quicumque uolumina tangis,
   his saltem uestra detur in urbe locus.
quoque magis faueas, haec non sunt edita ab ipso,
   sed quasi de domini funere rapta sui.
quicquid in his igitur uitii rude carmen habebit,
   emendaturus, si licuisset, eram.'[1]

The poem consists of fifteen books of hexameter

---

[1] *Tr.* 1, 7, 35–40. The friend to whom this letter was addressed
was probably Ovid's publisher. He had a garlanded bust of the
poet in his house and wore a ring engraved with his likeness—
and well he might, for Ovid was a best-seller.

verse, containing some two hundred and fifty stories of the transformations of men and women into animal, and other, shapes. It is arranged in a roughly chronological order, beginning with the creation of the world from Chaos and ending with the comet that appeared at the time of Caesar's murder and was popularly believed to be the new abode of his soul. In the first thirteen books almost all the tales have been taken from the rich storehouse of Greek mythology, but the last two books recount a majority of stories of native Italian origin.

The *Metamorphoses* is in fact a collection of *epyllia*, or short narrative poems, skilfully woven together so as to form a continuous work (*Met.* 1, 4, *carmen perpetuum*). The epyllion was a literary form developed during the Alexandrian Age, when epic on the Homeric pattern was out of favour. The form is represented in Greek literature by such poems as the *Hecale* of Callimachus, the *Hylas* and *Heracliscus* of Theocritus, the *Achilleis* of Bion and the *Europa* of Moschus. In Latin we can recognise as epyllia Catullus' *Peleus and Thetis*, the *Culex*, the *Ciris*, and the Aristaeus episode from Virgil's fourth *Georgic*. The distinguishing characteristics of the type are that it should be a narrative poem of moderate length containing speeches and passages of dialogue and usually at some point in its course a digression, contrasting with the main theme. The story of Io in *Met.* 1 provides a good example of an Ovidian epyllion, the digression there consisting of the tale of Pan and Syrinx. Other examples are the story of Narcissus in *Met.* 3 with its digression on Echo, the story of Ceres in *Met.* 5 with its digression on Arethusa; and there are many more. It has been estimated that about one third of the tales in the *Metamorphoses* are full-blown epyllia; the rest, like the *Hylas* of Theocritus, are epyllia that lack the characteristic element of a digression.[1]

What models did Ovid use in composing this lengthy poem? The question is hard to answer. Earlier works on this theme have not come down to us. We must be content with *a priori* arguments and the few shreds of ancient evidence that we possess. We know that Alexandrian writers were the first to make collections of stories of transformations and link them together in a continuous series, just as, much earlier, the Boeotian poet Hesiod had collected the traditional lore about the gods and worked it up in his *Theogony*. In the third or fourth century B.C. there appeared a poem called *Ornithogonia*, composed by one Boio, or Boios. In this the stories from mythology about transformations into birds were gathered together and re-told in verse; it was in fact a versified collection of the traditional Just So stories that explained how various species of birds came into being. Certainly in the third century B.C. the polymath Eratosthenes, best known as one of the founders of scientific geography, brought together the tales about transformations into stars and wrote them up in prose in his *Catasterismoi*. These were, so to speak, specialised works on particular aspects of the theme of metamorphosis. It was not until the second century B.C. that the theme was treated generally, by Nicander of Colophon in his *Heteroioumena*, a hexameter poem in five books. The next author to handle the subject was Parthenius of Nicaea, who was a friend of Cornelius Gallus and is said to have taught Virgil Greek; he composed a work,

[1] See M. M. Crump, *The Epyllion from Theocritus to Ovid*, p. 203.

whether in prose or verse is uncertain, entitled *Metamorphoses*. Finally there existed in Ovid's time another work with the same title by a certain Theodorus, about whom nothing is known beyond his name.

We may suppose that Ovid occasionally drew on Boio's poem when telling some of the many stories about the transformation of men into birds in his *Metamorphoses;* indeed Aemilius Macer of Verona wrote a Latin version of the *Ornithogonia* and Ovid remarks that he often listened to the poet reciting it (*Tr.* 4, 10, 43). As regards Nicander and Theodorus, the grammarian Probus (first century A.D.) states explicitly in a note on *Georgics* 1, 399 that in describing the origin of the halcyon Ovid follows Nicander in one place (*Met.* 11, 410 ff.) and Theodorus in another (*Met.* 7, 401-3). Further information is provided by the scholiast on Antoninus Liberalis, who wrote a *Collection of Metamorphoses* in Greek prose, probably during the Antonine age. The scholiast carefully notes the Alexandrian sources of various stories told in the *Collection*, and with this help it has been possible to show that Ovid follows Nicander in other passages too; it is a likely inference that Ovid's debt to him is considerable. •

It is also likely that Ovid had before him a prose handbook such as the *Bibliotheca* of Apollodorus, pupil of the great Alexandrian scholar Aristarchus, to which he could turn in order to refresh his memory on points of detail in Greek mythology, and which may well have provided him with a useful framework for the chronological arrangement of his own poem. For the legends of Italian origin in the later part of the poem he would have recourse to Ennius and Varro.

Finally, he would no doubt be acquainted with such Latin epyllia on the theme of metamorphosis as Cicero's *Halcyones*, Helvius Cinna's *Smyrna* and Licinius Calvus' *Io*; indeed the latter half of line 632 in *Met.* 1 is a reminiscence of a verse from this last poem.[1]

If there is doubt about the extent of Ovid's debt to predecessors whose works no longer survive, it is an easier task to determine the use which he made of masterpieces of Greek and Roman literature that have come down to us. It is evident, for example, that in his miniature *Aeneid, Met.* 13,623-14,574, he follows Virgil; that in Medea's monologue (*Met.* 7, 11 ff.) he has the Euripidean dramatic soliloquy in mind; that the opening of *Met.* 1 and the long speech of Pythagoras in *Met.* 15 are to some extent inspired by Lucretius; and that the Philemon and Baucis episode (*Met.* 8, 611 ff.) contains much that is borrowed from the *Hecale* of Callimachus. For apart from the broad use of models, Ovid sometimes introduces lines and phrases borrowed from other poets. For example, in *Met.* 1 line 9, *semina rerum* is a Lucretian echo; line 486 is translated from Callimachus; line 414 is a reminiscence of *Georgics* 1, 63; line 632, as we have seen, is an echo from Calvus. Such borrowings were an acknowledged part of the craft of ancient poetry. Sometimes they were introduced as a compliment to the original author; sometimes because the expression of an idea could not be bettered; more often to show that this was poetry 'in the tradition', or to enable the author to give a new twist of meaning to a memorable

---

[1] Calvus' *Io* is lost, but Servius on Virg. *Ecl.* 6, 47 quotes the line in question. It runs: 'a, uirgo infelix, herbis pasceris amaris'.

phrase. The reader would be expected to recognise the allusion. It would be wrong to regard the practice as mere plagiarism.

Like Virgil, Ovid would use his models in an original way, infusing something of himself into his borrowings from others. We have already noticed how he found his own meaning in a line of Varro Atacinus, and regarded this as an improvement on the original (see p. 12). It is reasonable to suppose that he treated his models in a similar spirit. Indeed the French scholar Lafaye, who made a special study of Ovid's debt to the Greeks, went so far as to say: 'De toutes les métamorphoses dont nous sommes témoins dans le poème d'Ovide, celle qu'il a fait subir à ses modèles n'est certainement pas la moins étonnante.'[1]

Even with the help of models and mythological handbooks the writing of such an ambitious work must have proved a formidable undertaking. But Ovid was not the man to shirk artistic difficulties. On the contrary, they stimulated his invention. We have only to think of how in his elegiacs he bound himself by the strict rule of the dissyllabic ending to the pentameter, and turned the restriction into a delight. Now one of the main difficulties that faced him in the composition of the *Metamorphoses* was that of passing smoothly from one story to the next so that the whole poem should give the appearance of continuity and fulfil his promise that it was to be a *carmen perpetuum*. If we consider the stories grouped together in *Met.* 1, we can form some idea of the problem Ovid had to solve; they are: the Creation, the Four Ages, the War of the Giants and the Gods, Lycaon, the Flood,

[1] *Les Métamorphoses d'Ovide et leurs Modèles Grecs*, Paris, 1904, p. 241.

Deucalion and Pyrrha, the killing of Python by Apollo, Apollo and Daphne, Io, Pan and Syrinx, Phaethon. There is no difficulty about the first two, for they follow on naturally; similarly the Flood is the consequence of Lycaon's sin, and Deucalion and Pyrrha are the sole survivors of the catastrophe; again, Apollo is the main actor both in the story of Python and in that of Daphne. The other tales, however, have no obvious connexion with their neighbours, and it is just here that we can test Ovid's skill in weaving them in. He accomplishes the transition from the Iron Age, last of the Four Ages, to the War of the Giants by the single line: 'neue foret terris securior arduus aether' (151). To lead on from the defeat of the Giants to Lycaon, he describes how the blood that the Giants shed in their fight with the Olympians fell on the earth and turned into human beings who despised the gods. Jupiter sees this race from heaven and is reminded of how Lycaon tried to murder him. To link Deucalion and Pyrrha with Python, he tells us that after the Flood animal life sprang up again from the mud left behind by the water as it receded, and that various monsters were brought into being, among them—Python. There is also a geographical connexion here, since Deucalion and Pyrrha landed on Mount Parnassus and it was on that mountain that Python lived. Finally, to pass from Daphne to Io, Ovid makes the other river-gods come to condole with Daphne's father after her transformation into a bay-tree. But Inachus, Io's father, was missing from their number. Why? we ask; and the story of Io gives the reason. Enough has been said to show that Ovid's transitions are skilfully managed. Quintilian indeed thought some of them over-ingenious, but excused Ovid on the ground that he was forced to give his work the appearance of unity (*Inst. Or.* 4, 1, 77).

No less striking than Ovid's adroitness in giving his poem continuity is the spirit in which he treats these traditional stories of the marvellous. Though many of them have their origin far back in human history in the first attempts of primitive man to explain the world about him, Ovid does not try to impart to them the least flavour of antiquity. There are few hints in the *Metamorphoses* of the archaism that Virgil exploited in his *Aeneid*. Ovid, who congratulated himself on his good fortune in being born into the Augustan age (see p. 13), treats his material in the spirit of that age. The gods in his poem are for the most part drawn on the same scale as the human beings. In the story of Daphne, Apollo reminds one of the conventional lover of Roman Elegy. The assembly of the gods in *Met.* 1 is a celestial Senate, Jupiter a divine Augustus. The minor gods of the Pantheon are called *plebs*, and the part of heaven inhabited by the major divinities is likened to the Palatine in Rome. Sometimes this modernity of treatment is also apparent in the poet's diction. Such usages as 'tantum spatii de monte' (*Met.* 1, 440), 'Naias una fuit' (691), 'in statione manebant' (627) would appear to be drawn from the language of everyday. 'Litem diremit' (21) and 'addicere' (617) are metaphors drawn from current legal phraseology. The poem abounds in new words that Ovid may well have coined; in *Met.* 1 for example, *innabilis* (16), *monticolae* (193), *dubitabile* (223), *hortamine* (277), *defrenato* (282), *indeiecta* (289), *populifer* (579). Again, Ovidian similes sometimes appear in modern dress; Apollo is compared to a *canis Gallicus*, a well-known breed of dog in Ovid's own day.

Allied to ˌthis modernity of spirit is the humour which every now and then enlivens the poem. Phoebus pursuing Daphne can yet find breath for a speech of considerable length and plead for a gentleman's agreement in the conduct of the race (510-11). Juno, gazing down from heaven and observing an odd-looking cloud, clearly not the result of natural causes, hastily looks about for Jupiter, and not finding him anywhere, jumps to the right conclusion. But humour is less characteristic of the *Metamorphoses* than wit, the unexpected combination of apparently disconnected or contradictory ideas. It is Ovid's delight in this that has won him most enemies among the critics. 'Nimium amator ingenii sui', says Quintilian, in a phrase that has set the tone for many later criticisms, though he adds: 'laudandus tamen in partibus' (*Inst. Or.* 10, 1, 88). 'Pueriles ineptias' is the younger Seneca's comment on the line 'nat lupus inter oues, fuluos uehit unda leones' (304) (*N.Q.* 3, 27, 13); his father pronounces judgement on Ovid in a similar strain: 'nescit quod bene cessit relinquere' (*Contr.* 9, 5, 17), and again, 'non ignorauit uitia sua, sed amauit' (*Contr.* 2, 2, 12). There is no denying the charge; Ovid is sometimes lacking in self-criticism. It was for example an error of judgement to make Marsyas say, while being flayed alive, 'quid me mihi detrahis?' 'Why do you tear me from myself?'[1] But not every Ovidian arrow overshoots the mark. What could be neater than his description of Envy (*Met.* 2, 796): 'uixque tenet lacrimas quia nil lacrimabile cernit'? What more beautiful than the picture of Galatea, the statue, opening her eyes at the kiss of Pygmalion (*Met.* 10, 292 ff.):

[1] *Met.* 6, 385; quoted by W. C. Summers in the Introduction to his edition of *Met.* 8.

'dataque oscula uirgo
sensit et erubuit, timidumque ad lumina lumen
attollens, pariter cum caelo uidit amantem.'?

In *Met.* 1 there are relatively few examples, but the
following might be quoted: 355 'nos duo turba
sumus'; 584 'fletibus auget aquas'; 629 'ante oculos Io,
quamuis auersus, habebat'; and Argus' epitaph in
720-1.

The poetry of wit is perhaps an acquired taste, but
few will deny Ovid's mastery of the quotable phrase,
his power of expressing an old thought in a new or
more succinct manner. Here are some examples:
'leue fit quod bene fertur onus' (*Am.* 1, 2, 10); 'ut
ameris amabilis esto' (*Ars* 2, 107); 'fas est et ab hoste
doceri' (*Met.* 4, 428); 'medio tutissimus ibis' (2, 137);
'rudis indigestaque moles' (1,7). It was this happy
gift that made Landor declare that 'Ovid with all his
levity has more unobtrusively sage verses than any, be
he Roman or Athenian.'

Undeniable too is Ovid's power of graphic descrip-
tion. He was gifted with a lively and sensuous imagina-
tion. The abstract in itself had little hold on him; he
must realise it and translate it into physical terms.
Hence the frequent personifications in his poetry.
Envy, Hunger, Sleep, and Fame are turned into human
figures, grotesque perhaps but none the less alive.
Moreover he looked out upon the external world with
unusually alert perceptions. When Icarus flies too near
the sun and the wax on his wings begins to melt, we
read:

'rapidi uicinia solis
mollit odoratas, pennarum uincula, ceras.'
(*Met.* 8, 226)

Here the adjective *odoratas* could not be bettered, for the smell of wax is only apparent when heat has been applied to it. Describing a boy diving into a pool Ovid writes:

> 'ille cauis uelox applauso corpore palmis
> desilit in latices'
>
> *(Met.* 4, 352)

and the simple detail of the diver clapping his side with hollowed hands before plunging in is a piece of observation that brings the description to life, especially as in the Latin one can hear the sound of the action. Or again, in a simile about pine woods occur these lines:

> 'qualia succinctis, ubi trux insibilat Eurus,
> murmura pinetis fiunt.'
>
> *(Met.* 15, 603)

Of this Henry remarks (*Aeneidea*, vol. 1, p. 618): 'Whoever has been in a pine wood will require no further comment on *succincta*, in its literal application to the female dress. A pine wood is indeed a wood of bare legs. Let no one say that Ovid is not a poet, or subscribe to Dryden's most unjust opinion of him. He was a more natural, more genial, more cordial, more imaginative, more playful poet not only than Dryden, but than our author [i.e. Virgil], or any other Latin poet.' In Ovid, sensuous imagination and accurate observation combine to give his poetry a clarity and definition of outline that contrast sharply with the vaguer and more evocative manner of Virgil. The pictorial detail in Ovid sometimes recalls the wall paintings in Roman villas, known to us from those that have been preserved in Pompeii. Ovid grew up

among such works of art and they must have influen-
ced his imagination strongly. Conversely, painters in
later ages were enthralled by Ovid's exuberant fancy
and drew inspiration for mythological pictures from
the pages of his *Metamorphoses.*

A remarkable feature of Ovid's descriptive style is
his use of 'theme and variation' (see note on line 85).
He takes an idea and expresses it in a variety of ways
in successive phrases or sentences, drawing out all its
implications. This is a characteristic of Virgil's style
too, but Ovid carries it even further.[1] Many examples
are to be found in *Met.* 1. For instance, the lines:

'iamque mare et tellus nullum discrimen habebant;
omnia pontus erat, derant quoque litora ponto'
(291-2)

consist of three sentences each expressing the same
thought. Or again, lines 89-93:

'aurea prima satast aetas, quae uindice nullo,
sponte sua, sine lege, fidem rectumque colebat.
poena metusque aberant, nec uerba minantia fixo
aere ligabantur, nec supplex turba timebat
iudicis ora sui, sed erant sine uindice tuti'

are really an elaboration of a single idea seen from
several angles. Such elaboration is usually labelled
'rhetorical', and the label is regarded as explanation
enough. The truth is that rhetoricians taught this
method of expansion for the good reason that they
were training men to speak to an audience, not to

---

[1] Lafaye, editor of the Budé *Metamorphoses,* has happily
described this device in Ovid's own words, taken from *A.A.*
2, 128: 'ille referre aliter saepe solebat idem'.—See also Postgate,
Select Elegies of Propertius, pp. lxxix-lxxxi.

write for an unseen reader. Hearing is a less sure
process than sight; it takes longer to communicate an
idea through the ear than through the eye. Hence the
necessity for varied repetition. Poets too, no less than
orators, had a listening (and applauding) audience in
mind as they wrote, so that Ovid can say:

> 'in tenebris numerosos ponere gestus
> quodque legas nulli scribere carmen, idem est'

'To write poetry which you can read to no one is the
same as dancing in the dark' (*Ex P.* 4, 2, 33-4).

But it is, after all, the vitality of Ovid's poetry that
never ceases to astonish. In all his large output, if we
except some of the poems written in exile, there is
hardly a dull page. The *Metamorphoses* are the best
witness to this vitality. It needed a poet of genius to
bring to convincing life such an accumulation of
strange stories. The mere planning of the work and its
orderly arrangement must have been a considerable
labour, let alone the task of composition which Ovid
carried through to the end with unflagging invention.
And what, it may be asked, has all this labour accom-
plished? If we believe that the aim of poetry is to give
pleasure, Ovid's pains have been amply justified, for
few of the world's great books can have given more
pleasure to a larger number of readers and listeners
than the *Metamorphoses*. If on the other hand we
wish not only to be pleased but to be edified, we can
take comfort from the words of Ovid's greatest
translator, Arthur Golding:

> 'For this do learned persons deeme of Ouid's
>   present worke:
> That in no one of all his bookes the which he
>   wrate, do lurke

Mo darke and secret mysteries, mo counselles wise
   and sage,
Mo good ensamples, mo reproofes of uice in youth
   and age.'

Ovid's golden treasury will have something for every-
one. His book sings of the manifold variety of life,
telling us that the world is full of beauty and wonder,
that life is good and to be enjoyed.

C. OTHER WORKS OF OVID

Apart from the *Metamorphoses* and the *Halieutica*, a
short fragment from a didactic poem written during
his banishment on the subject of the fisherman's art,
Ovid's other extant works are composed in elegiac
couplets. They are:

1. *Amores*. A collection of love poems telling the
story of the poet's attachment to a girl whom he calls
Corinna. We do not know her real name; it is possible
that she was an imaginary figure. The work was origin-
ally published in five books not long after 16 B.C.,
but later Ovid revised it and reduced the number of
books to three. It is this second edition that we
possess. Ovid, who calls himself 'tenerorum lusor
amorum' (*Tr.* 4, 10, 1), treats the theme of love in the
Amores with a light-hearted playfulness reminiscent of
New Comedy and contrasting strongly with the
devouring passion of Catullus or Propertius and the
romantic melancholy of Tibullus. The contrast can be
clearly seen from a comparison of Catullus 76 'si qua
recordanti' and 85 'odi et amo' with *Am.* 3,11. The
most celebrated poems in the collection are 1, 13, the
ancestor of the medieval *Aubade*; the elegy for
Corinna's parrot (2, 6), which is worth comparing with

Catullus on Lesbia's *passer* and Statius *Siluae* 2, 4; and the elegy on the death of Tibullus (3, 9). But much else of beauty can be found. The verse is highly polished and elaborated with delicate craftsmanship. The work is admirable light poetry.

2. *Heroides*. Imaginary letters written by the heroines of antiquity to their absent lovers. 1-15 were first published, then much later Ovid added the double letters, 16-21, where the men also write. Ovid claims to have invented the genre ('ignotum hoc aliis ille nouauit opus' *A.A.* 3, 346), and there is no reason to doubt him. From the epithet by which he describes the heroines in *Tr.* 1, 6, 33 'prima locum sanctas Heroidas inter haberes', it is evident that he did not regard the work as light poetry; apart from the letters of Helen and Paris, the tone is serious and reveals a depth of feeling that is generally absent from the *Amores*. The letters were probably designed as dramatic monologues to be rendered in character (cf. *A.A.* 3, 345 'uel tibi composita cantetur epistula uoce'). The epistolary form is a convenient device. Ovid has been careful to give each heroine a character of her own. Narrative forms a considerable part of most of the letters and this too helps to avoid the sameness inherent in the subject of the whole collection. Pope's *Eloisa to Abelard* and Julia's letter in Byron's *Don Juan* (Canto 1, stanzas 191-197) are very reminiscent of the *Heroides*. The work was much admired in the last century; Merivale declares that 'the Loves of the Heroines is the most elevated and refined in sentiment of all elegiac compositions of the Romans'.[1]

3. *De Medicamine Faciei*. A witty fragment on the subject of cosmetics, chiefly remarkable for the

[1] *A History of the Romans under the Empire*, chap. 41 *ad fin.*

ingenuity Ovid shows in versifying recipes for skin lotions, face creams etc.—their ingredients and quantities. Didactic poetry of this kind was popular in the Augustan age, as we know, for example, from Horace's skit on cookery in *Satires* 2, 4. Ovid in this work, as in the *Ars Amatoria* and the *Remedia Amoris*, parodies the serious didactic style.

4. *Ars Amatoria.* A manual of instruction for philanderers in the conduct and etiquette of an affair. It was published soon after 1 B.C. in three books, the first two addressed to men, the third to the fair sex. The poem is a *jeu d'esprit*; 'lusus habet finem' Ovid remarks, towards the conclusion (3, 809). It displays psychological insight enlivened by sparkling wit. Stories from legend told with consummate skill illustrate the teaching and add variety; e.g. Theseus and Ariadne (1, 525 ff.), Daedalus and Icarus (2, 21 ff.), Cephalus and Procris (3, 687 ff.). Though the *Ars* has often been censured for its immorality, it contains none of the grossness that sometimes disfigures the pages of Catullus, Horace, Martial and Juvenal. It does not make sin attractive. The reader is entertained but not allured by the cynical view of love that Ovid here professes, and is left with the impression that the brilliant and brittle world of Ovid's imagining is in essence nothing but vanity and vexation of spirit. The poem in fact has the effect of satire. Macaulay regarded it as Ovid's masterpiece.

5. *Remedia Amoris.* Published after the *Ars* and before A.D. 2. It is in some sort an apology for the earlier poem. The manner is the same, but here Ovid exerts his ingenuity to show the various ways in which the lover may rid himself of his passion. As before, precept is illustrated by story and diversified by lively

description. The work falls a little below the level of the *Ars*, but makes very agreeable reading.

6. *Fasti*. A poem based on the Roman calendar, in which Ovid describes the traditional festivals and rituals and tells the stories relating to them. Its composition was interrupted by his banishment (*Tr.* 2, 552). Six books, dealing in order with the months of January to June, have come down to us, but it would appear from *Tr.* 2, 549 that Ovid wrote twelve ('sex ego Fastorum scripsi totidemque libellos'). The missing six either have been lost, or were in such a rough state that the poet's executors suppressed them. The original dedication was to Augustus, for Ovid no doubt hoped to find favour by a work which was in line with his policy of fostering the traditional religion. On the death of Augustus it was re-dedicated to Germanicus. Apart from its great charm as a work of art, the *Fasti* is a mine of information about Roman cults and observances and of the highest interest to students of ancient religion. It was inspired by the *Aetia* of Callimachus.

7. Poems from exile: (a). *Tristia*. Five books of letters in verse sent to his wife and anonymous friends in Rome during the years A.D. 8-12. Book 2 is a long letter to Augustus presenting an elaborate defence of the *Ars Amatoria*. (b). *Epistulae ex Ponto*. Four books of letters written during the period A.D. 12-16 in the same vein as the *Tristia*, though with the difference that Ovid's friends are now addressed by name.

Ovid's purpose in composing these letters was not only to appeal to the compassion of his friends and persuade them to do their best to gain some mitigation of his sentence, but also to write poetry of a new and original kind. He paints a gloomy picture of his manner of life at Tomi, of the climate and the inhabitants; he mingles exaggerated praise of Augustus with appeals to his clemency; he repeatedly complains about the hardness of his fate, his ill-health and the barbarity of his surroundings. But in spite of a certain monotony, there is much fine poetry among the letters from banishment. The verse shows little falling off in technique. The old facility remains, though chastened by suffering and not seldom strengthened by a new depth of feeling.

(c) *Ibis*. A long imprecatory poem directed against an unknown enemy who was trying to make capital out of the poet's ruin, and modelled on the lost *Ibis* of Callimachus, in which he inveighed against his rival Apollonius Rhodius. The ibis was a bird notorious in antiquity for its unclean habits (see Strabo 17, 823). Ovid's poem is crammed with recondite mythological allusions, for he calls down on the head of his enemy a host of disasters suffered by legendary figures of the past. Housman regarded the first 250 lines as a masterpiece,[1] but thereafter the long rigmarole of curses makes for the most part dreary reading.

D. THE OVIDIAN HEXAMETER

Readers of Ovid and Virgil are at once conscious of a difference in the handling of the Latin hexameter by the two poets. It is well-known that this difference resolves itself into two main questions: (i) the movement of the line; (ii) the frequency of elision. Ovid's line is more dactylic than Virgil's and has fewer elisions; moreover his elisions tend to be light ones.

[1] *Journal of Philology* xxxv (1920), p. 317: 'Ovid has written no passage of equal length which has equal merit.'

It seems worth while to try to support this general impression by a detailed comparison of the practice of the two poets.

I. *Spondees and dactyls in the first four feet*

What then are Ovid's favourite arrangements of dactyls and spondees in the first four feet of the hexameter, and how does his practice here compare with Virgil's? In this enquiry we look at their hexameter lines purely from the point of view of metrical scheme, excluding all questions of caesura and elision.

Virgil's practice has been worked out by Lederer for the whole of the *Aeneid*. The percentages for the nine most important combinations are as follows[1]:

1. DSSS 14·3% e.g. *parcere subiectis et debellare superbos*
2. DDSS 12 % *arma uirumque cano Troiae qui primus ab oris*
3. DSDS 11·2% *Italiam fato profugus Lauinaque uenit*
4. SDSS 9·5% *tantae molis erat Romanam condere gentem*
5. SSSS 7·1% *ibant obscuri sola sub nocte per umbram*
6. DDDS 6·8% *quique sui memores alios fecere merendo*
7. SSDS 5·9% *si non pertaesum thalami taedaeque fuisset*
8. SDDS 5·8% *uenit summa dies et ineluctabile tempus*
9. DSSD 5·7% *talia flammato secum dea corde uolutans.*

---

[1] The figures have been taken from Winbolt, *Latin Hexameter Verse*, pp. 113 f.

The figures showing Ovid's preference in the first book of the *Metamorphoses* are given below. There would probably be alterations of emphasis if the count were extended to include all fifteen books of the poem, but I do not believe they would be big enough to upset the broad conclusions drawn from an examination of only one book:

1. DSSS 14·3% e.g. *nullus adhuc mundo prae-bebat lumina Titan*
2. DSSD 12·7% *nullaque mortales, praeter sua, litora norant*
3. DSDS 11·5% *nec noua crescendo reparabat cornua Phoebe*
4. DDSS 11 % *congeriem secuit sectamque in membra coegit*
5. DDSD 10·4% *ad mea perpetuum deducite tempora carmen*
6. DSDD 9·1% *Eurus ad Auroram Nabataeaque regna recessit*
7. DDDS 8·9% *nec renouatus ager grauidis canebat aristis*
8. DDDD 5·8% *sanguineaque manu crepitantia concutit arma*
9. SDSD 4·1% *mulcebant Zephyri natos sine semine flores*

It will be evident at once that there is much more dactylic movement in Ovid, though he agrees with Virgil in making DSSS a staple arrangement. In Ovid, however, this is followed by DSSD which stands at the bottom of the Virgilian list. Virgil's preference for SDSS is rejected by Ovid; there are only thirty-one lines of this type in *Met.* 1. Ovid also rejects Virgil's use of lines beginning with four spondees (SSSS); there are only nine examples in *Met.* 1.

But the difference between the two poets is most marked in their treatment of the first and the fourth foot. Of the nine favourite types of Ovidian line cited above, eight begin with a dactyl and only one with a spondee. Virgil on the other hand has dactylic first foot in five examples, spondaic in four. As regards the fourth foot, Virgil has a spondee in that place in eight out of the nine types, whereas in Ovid the proportion is five dactylic fourth feet to four spondaic. In other words, Ovid prefers to begin his line with a dactyl; Virgil holds a more even balance between spondaic and dactylic beginning. Virgil prefers to have a spondee in the fourth foot; Ovid keeps a more even balance.

II. *Elision*

If we compare the frequency of elision in Virgil and Ovid the difference is equally marked. An American scholar, R. G. Kent, totted up and classified the elisions in four books of the *Aeneid* (1, 4, 7 and 12) and four of the *Metamorphoses* (1, 5, 10 and 15). Tabulated details of his results can be found in his article 'Likes and Dislikes in Elision' (*Transactions of the American Philological Association*, 54, pp. 86-97). Here it is only necessary to give a summary.

Elisions may be divided into five classes:
(1) aphaeresis of *est*.
(2) elision of *-que*, including *quoque*, *quisque* etc.
(3) elision of a vowel followed by a final *m*.
(4) elision of a short final vowel (excluding class 2, of course).
(5) elision of a long final vowel, or diphthong.

For the sake of convenience Kent refers to these five classes as respectively: T, Q, M, S, and L.

To sum up his results we may say that Virgil has rather more than twice as many elisions as Ovid. In reading the *Aeneid* one would expect to find on the average one elision in every two lines; in reading the *Metamorphoses*, about one elision in every four lines. The preference of the two poets for the various types of elision is interesting. Virgil is very sparing in his use of T(3%), but employs the four other forms about equally, with a slight preference for M (27%). Ovid, on the other hand, dislikes L and M (4% and 10% respectively), uses T and S about equally (22%) and has a strong preference for Q (42%).

It is worth noting that longish passages can occur in the *Metamorphoses* with no elision at all; e.g. *Met.* 1, 292-313, 446-463.

III. *Bucolic Diaeresis*

We have seen that Ovid has a slight preference for a dactyl in the fourth foot. We should therefore expect to find more examples of Bucolic Diaeresis in his hexameters than in Virgil's. By Bucolic Diaeresis is meant here the rhythm that occurs when the fourth foot is a dactyl and at the same time the end of that foot corresponds with the end of a word, e.g.

4
'uesper et occiduo quae/litora/ sole tepescunt

4
ut lenita dea est, uul/tus capit/ illa priores.'

Whereas *Aen.* 1 (756 lines) yields some 95 examples of this, there are about 175 in *Met.* 1 (779 lines).[1] The rhythm is characteristic of Ovid, and in this respect at

[1] Excluding examples containing elision between the fourth and fifth feet and those where a preposition goes with its noun, e.g. *Met.* 1, 26.

least, as in that of dactylic movement, his hexameter comes closer to the Greek hexameter than Virgil's does.

IV. *Trochaic Caesura in the fourth foot*

As a further consequence of Ovid's liking for a dactyl in the fourth foot we find that he not infrequently has a trochaic caesura there. For example, in the line 'et liquidum spisso secreuit ab aere caelum', there is a trochaic, or weak, caesura after the final syllable of 'secreuit'. Further examples can be found in *Met.* 1 lines 12, 31, 36, 55 etc.; and in consecutive lines, 329-30, 341-2, 583-4. This rhythm is avoided altogether in the Greek hexameter. Virgil uses it sparingly, but it would appear to be commoner in Ovid. In *Aen.* 1 there are twenty-six examples; in *Met.* 1 as many as sixty-three.[1]

E.   SOME ENGLISH TRANSLATIONS OF THE *METAMORPHOSES*

The first complete translation of the *Metamorphoses* into English verse was undertaken by Arthur Golding. In 1565 he published the first four books, and the reception accorded to them encouraged him to translate the rest. The complete work appeared in 1567. Golding came of a family of Essex landed gentry, moved in good society in London and was a friend of Sir Philip Sidney. He was an assiduous translator. He published versions of Caesar's *Commentaries* and Seneca's *De Beneficiis*, and occupied himself in making available to English readers the works of the theologians Calvin and Beza, for he had strong Puritan leanings. His religious convictions show themselves

[1] See J. J. Hartman, *De Ovidio Poeta*, Leyden, 1905, pp. 11 ff.

in the dedicatory epistle prefixed to his *Metamorphoses*. There he provides a summary of all the stories to be told and shows considerable ingenuity in giving each one a moral interpretation.

As the metre of his translation he chose the 'fourteener', a long swinging line of fourteen syllables, well adapted to reproduce Ovid's quickly moving narrative, but yet, by a certain roughness inherent in the nature of so long a line, unable to do full justice to the polish and finesse of the Ovidian hexameter. But his translation is admirable in its vigour and directness, and delightful for its homely and vivid vocabulary. His version of the simile of the greyhound and the hare, quoted in the note on line 533, is an excellent example of these qualities. On the whole his translation is faithful, but he often expands the Latin, as when he renders *nec supplex turba timebat iudicis ora sui* as 'There was no man would crouch or creepe to Judge with cap in hand', or *proque toro* as 'And in the sted of costlie couch and good soft fether-bed'.

It has been shown that Shakespeare knew Golding's work. Prospero's speech in the *Tempest* beginning 'Ye elves of hills, brooks, standing lakes, and groves' is a striking adaptation of Golding's version of *Met.* 7, 197-206:

'Ye Ayres and windes: ye Elves of Hilles, of
   Brookes, of Woods alone,
Of standing Lakes and of the Night, approche ye
   everychone.
Through helpe of whom (the crooked bankes much
   wondring at the thing)
I have compelled streames to run cleane backward
   to their spring.

By charmes I make the calme Seas rough, and make
the rough Seas plaine,
And cover all the Skie with Cloudes and chase them
thence againe.
By charmes I rayse and lay the windes and burst the
Vipers jaw,
And from the bowels of the Earth both stones and
trees doe drawe.
Whole woods and Forestes I remove; I make the
Mountaines shake,
And even the Earth it selfe to grone and fearfully to
quake.
I call up dead men from their graves.'[1]

In recent times Golding has found a fervent
admirer in the American poet Ezra Pound, who in
his *ABC of Reading* (p. 113) writes: 'I do not honestly
think that anyone can know anything about the art of
lucid narrative in English, or let us say about the
history of the development of English narrative-
writing (verse or prose) without seeing the whole of the
volume [Golding's *Metamorphoses*].' And a little later
in the same passage Pound calls the work 'the most
beautiful book in the language.'

The next Englishman to be fond enough of Ovid's
Metamorphoses to try his hand at a full-scale verse
rendering was George Sandys, youngest son of
Edwin Sandys, Archbishop of York, and, unlike
Golding, a traveller and a man of action. In 1621 he
sailed for America as the colonial treasurer of the
Virginia Company, and during his stay in the New
World he finished his rendering of the *Metamorphoses*,

---

[1] Quoted from *Ovid and the Elizabethans* by F. S. Boas (p. 6),
published by the English Association in 1947.

five books of which he had already published before
leaving England. He tells us that two of the remainder
were completed 'amongst the roaring of the seas', and
one cannot help remembering that Ovid himself
wrote poetry on board the ship that carried him to his
long exile.[1] A revised edition of the complete work,
dedicated to Charles I and provided with learned notes
by the translator, was published in 1632.

Sandys chose the heroic couplet as his metre, and
this, though a less tractable medium than Golding's
fourteener, gives a better representation of the smooth-
ness and elegance of the Ovidian hexameter. It was
Sandys' aim to make his version as far as possible line
for line, and he was remarkably successful in this; he
translates *Met.* 1 in 780 lines, exceeding his original by
one line only. As a good example of the quality of his
verse and one which at the same time allows compari-
son with Golding, here is his version of the hare and
greyhound simile:

'As when a Hare the speedy Grey-hound spies,
His Feet for Prey, she hers for Safety plies;
Now bears he up, now, now he hopes to fetch her;
And with his Snowt extended strains to catch her:
Not knowing whether caught or no, she slips
Out of his wide-stretched Jaws and touching Lips.'

Sandys' rendering, as usual line for line, is both more
compact and more faithful than Golding's, which takes
ten fourteeners to represent six hexameters.

Sidney Lee, in the *Dictionary of National Biography*,
summarises his achievement thus: 'Sandys possessed

---

[1] See *Tr.* 1, 11, 7–8:
    'quod facerem uersus inter fera murmura ponti,
      Cycladas Aegaeas obstipuisse puto.'

exceptional metrical dexterity, and the refinement with which he handled the couplet entitles him to a place beside Denham and Waller. In a larger measure than either of them he probably helped to develop the capacity of heroic rhyme. He was almost the first writer to vary the caesura efficiently and by adroitly balancing one couplet against another he anticipated some of the effects which Dryden and Pope brought to perfection.' Dryden read Sandys' *Ovid* as a boy, and in the preface to the *Fables* refers to 'the ingenious and learned Sandys' as 'the best versifier of the former age'. Pope too read Sandys in his young days and Spence records that he 'liked him extremely'.[1] In a satirical ballad called *Sandys' Ghost* he attacks the contributors (though he himself was one of them) to a new translation of the *Metamorphoses* designed to supersede Sandys' rendering, by then about a hundred years old.

This new version was published by Sir Samuel Garth in 1717. The contributors to it included Dryden, Addison, Pope, Congreve, Croxall and Rowe. Dryden's translation of *Met.* 1, which had first appeared in *Examen Poeticum* (1693), is here reprinted. It is not one of Dryden's best renderings, though here and there one comes upon memorable lines and phrases. However Dryden's own opinion of this and the other translations from the *Metamorphoses* in *Examen Poeticum* was high. 'They appear to me,' he writes, 'the best of all my Endeavours in this kind.' In fact he is not as faithful to the Latin as either of his predecessors. Here for example is his version of the simile already quoted:

[1] L. G. Sherburn, *The Early Career of Alexander Pope*, Oxford, 1934, p. 83.

'As when th' impatient Greyhound slipt from far,
Bounds o're the Glebe, to course the fearful Hare,
She in her speed does all her safety lay;
And he with double speed pursues the Prey;
O're-runs her at the sitting turn, and licks
His chaps in vain, and blows upon the Flix,
She scapes, and for the neighb'ring Covert strives,
And gaining shelter, doubts if yet she lives.'

Shorter than Golding, it is two lines longer than
Sandys, and yet scamps some of the Latin to introduce
ideas of Dryden's own. But granted this, the transla-
tion is vivid enough, and in the fifth and sixth lines
there is a glimpse of a homely vocabulary reminiscent
of Golding at his best. An even clearer picture of the
merits and defects of Dryden's approach is provided
by the following lines (= *Met.* 1, 335-342):

'His writhen Shell he takes; whose narrow vent
Grows by degrees into a large extent;
Then gives it breath; the blast, with doubling sound,
Runs the wide Circuit of the World around.
The Sun first heard it, in his early East,
And met the rattling Eccho's in the West.
The Waters, listning to the Trumpets roar,
Obey the Summons, and forsake the Shoar.'

This is fine poetry. Dryden makes the reader hear the
distant reverberations of Triton's horn. It catches the
spirit of the Latin admirably, but omits many Ovidian
details. This is Dryden's general practice throughout
the book; he is faithful to the spirit, but not to the
letter. It is probably fair to say that he has reproduced
the tone and accent of Ovid more closely than either of
his predecessors, although they are more conscienti-
ous translators than he. 'Perhaps too, he was more

according to my Genius' Dryden had said of Ovid. There is no doubt of it. There are certain points of resemblance between the cultural climate of Augustan Rome and that of Restoration England.[1] Dryden and Ovid are both the mirrors of their age. They are both in love with wit and the pointed turn of phrase. They both excel in narrative verse. So when Dryden renders Ovid, he can remain himself and still be Ovidian. He can not only reproduce Ovidian epigram but can father epigrams of his own on Ovid, and no one who did not know the original could tell the difference. For example, he translates *Met.* 1, 6 as 'One was the Face of Nature, *if a Face*'. '*Stubborn as the Mettal were the Men*' he says of the Iron Age. When Inachus does not recognise Io in her new shape, Dryden gives:

> 'Ev'n Inachus himself was ignorant;
> *And in his Daughter did his Daughter want.*' (642)

And when Mercury cuts off the head of Argus of the many eyes, we read:

> 'Down from the Rock fell the dissever'd head,
> *Opening its Eyes in Death*, and falling bled.' (718/9)

The lines or phrases in italics are all embellishments added by Dryden, and yet they ring so true to Ovid's manner that perhaps he would have applauded their inclusion.

[1] See Mark van Doren, *The Poetry of John Dryden*, Cambridge, 1931, p. 10.

P. OVIDI NASONIS

METAMORPHOSEON

LIBER PRIMVS

Prologue

In noua fert animus mutatas dicere formas
corpora: di, coeptis — nam uos mutastis et illas —
adspirate meis primaque ab origine mundi
ad mea perpetuum deducite tempora carmen.

Chaos

ante mare et terras et quod tegit omnia caelum   5
unus erat toto naturae uultus in orbe,
quem dixere Chaos — rudis indigestaque moles
nec quicquam nisi pondus iners congestaque eodem
non bene iunctarum discordia semina rerum.
nullus adhuc mundo praebebat lumina Titan,   10
nec noua crescendo reparabat cornua Phoebe,
nec circumfuso pendebat in aere Tellus
ponderibus librata suis, nec bracchia longo
margine terrarum porrexerat Amphitrite.
utque erat et tellus illic et pontus et aer,   15
sic erat instabilis tellus, innabilis unda,
lucis egens aer. nulli sua forma manebat
obstabatque aliis aliud, quia corpore in uno
frigida pugnabant calidis, umentia siccis,
mollia cum duris, sine pondere habentia pondus.   20

The Creation of the World

hanc deus et melior litem natura diremit;
nam caelo terras et terris abscidit undas
et liquidum spisso secreuit ab aere caelum.
quae postquam euoluit caecoque exemit aceruo,
25 dissociata locis concordi pace ligauit.
ignea conuexi uis et sine pondere caeli
emicuit summaque locum sibi fecit in arce;
proximus est aer illi leuitate locoque;
densior his tellus elementaque grandia traxit
30 et pressast grauitate sua; circumfluus umor
ultima possedit solidumque coercuit orbem.
sic ubi dispositam quisquis fuit ille deorum
congeriem secuit sectamque in membra coegit,
principio terram, ne non aequalis ab omni
35 parte foret, magni speciem glomerauit in orbis.
tum freta diffudit rapidisque tumescere uentis
iussit et ambitae circumdare litora terrae.
addidit et fontes et stagna immensa lacusque,
fluminaque obliquis cinxit decliuia ripis,
40 quae diuersa locis partim sorbentur ab ipsa,
in mare perueniunt partim campoque recepta
liberioris aquae pro ripis litora pulsant.
iussit et extendi campos, subsidere ualles,
fronde tegi siluas, lapidosos surgere montes.
45 utque duae dextra caelum totidemque sinistra
parte secant zonae (quintast ardentior illis),
sic onus inclusum numero distinxit eodem
cura dei, totidemque plagae tellure premuntur.
quarum quae mediast, non est habitabilis aestu;
50 nix tegit alta duas; totidem inter utrumque locauit
temperiemque dedit mixta cum frigore flamma.
imminet his aer; qui, quantost pondere terrae
pondus aquae leuius, tantost onerosior igni.

illic et nebulas, illic consistere nubes
iussit et humanas motura tonitrua mentes   55
et cum fulminibus facientes fulgora uentos.
his quoque non passim mundi fabricator habendum
aera permisit: uix nunc obsistitur illis,
cum sua quisque regant diuerso flamina tractu,
quin lanient mundum; tantast discordia fratrum.   60
Eurus ad auroram Nabataeaque regna recessit
Persidaque et radiis iuga subdita matutinis;
uesper et occiduo quae litora sole tepescunt
proxima sunt Zephyro; Scythiam septemque Triones
horrifer inuasit Boreas; contraria tellus   65
nubibus assiduis pluuiaque madescit ab Austro.
haec super imposuit liquidum et grauitate carentem
aethera nec quicquam terrenae faecis habentem.
uix ita limitibus dissaepserat omnia certis
cum quae pressa diu massa latuere sub illa   70
sidera coeperunt toto efferuescere caelo.
neu regio foret ulla suis animalibus orba,
astra tenent caeleste solum formaeque deorum,
cesserunt nitidis habitandae piscibus undae,
terra feras cepit, uolucres agitabilis aer.   75

The Creation of Man

sanctius his animal mentisque capacius altae
derat adhuc et quod dominari in cetera posset.
natus homost; siue hunc diuino semine fecit
ille opifex rerum, mundi melioris origo,
siue recens tellus seductaque nuper ab alto   80
aethere cognati retinebat semina caeli;
quam satus Iapeto mixtam pluuialibus undis
finxit in effigiem moderantum cuncta deorum.
pronaque cum spectent animalia cetera terram,
os homini sublime dedit caelumque uidere   85

iussit et erectos ad sidera tollere uultus.
sic modo quae fuerat rudis et sine imagine **tellus**
induit ignotas hominum conuersa figuras.

The Four Ages

   aurea prima satast aetas, quae uindice nullo,
90 sponte sua, sine lege, fidem rectumque colebat.
poena metusque aberant, nec uerba minantia fixo
aere ligabantur, nec supplex turba timebat
iudicis ora sui, sed erant sine uindice tuti.
nondum caesa suis, peregrinum ut uiseret orbem,
95 montibus in liquidas pinus descenderat undas,
nullaque mortales, praeter sua, litora norant.
nondum praecipites cingebant oppida fossae;
non tuba derecti, non aeris cornua flexi,
non galeae, non ensis erat: sine militis usu
100 mollia securae peragebant otia gentes.
ipsa quoque immunis rastroque intacta nec ullis
saucia uomeribus per se dabat omnia tellus;
contentique cibis nullo cogente creatis
arbuteos fetus montanaque fraga legebant
105 cornaque et in duris haerentia mora rubetis
et quae deciderant patula Iouis arbore glandes.
uer erat aeternum, placidique tepentibus auris
mulcebant zephyri natos sine semine flores.
mox etiam fruges tellus inarata ferebat,
110 nec renouatus ager grauidis canebat aristis.
flumina iam lactis, iam flumina nectaris ibant,
flauaque de uiridi stillabant ilice mella.
   postquam Saturno tenebrosa in Tartara misso
sub Ioue mundus erat, subiit argentea proles,
115 auro deterior, fuluo pretiosior aere.
Iuppiter antiqui contraxit tempora ueris
perque hiemes aestusque et inaequales autumnos

et breue uer spatiis exegit quattuor annum.
tum primum siccis aer feruoribus ustus
canduit, et uentis glacies adstricta pependit.   120
tum primum subiere domos (domus antra fuerunt
et densi frutices et uinctae cortice uirgae).
semina tum primum longis Cerealia sulcis
obruta sunt, pressique iugo gemuere iuuenci.
    tertia post illam successit aenea proles,   125
saeuior ingeniis et ad horrida promptior arma,
non scelerata tamen. de durost ultima ferro.
protinus inrupit uenae peioris in aeuum
omne nefas: fugere pudor uerumque fidesque;
in quorum subiere locum fraudesque dolique   130
insidiaeque et uis et amor sceleratus habendi.
uela dabat uentis (nec adhuc bene nouerat illos)
nauita; quaeque diu steterant in montibus altis
fluctibus ignotis insultauere carinae.
communemque prius, ceu lumina solis et auras,   135
cautus humum longo signauit limite mensor.
nec tantum segetes alimentaque debita diues
poscebatur humus, sed itumst in uiscera terrae
quasque recondiderat Stygiisque admouerat umbris
effodiuntur opes, inritamenta malorum.   140
iamque nocens ferrum ferroque nocentius aurum
prodierat; prodit bellum, quod pugnat utroque
sanguineaque manu crepitantia concutit arma.
uiuitur ex rapto; non hospes ab hospite tutus,
non socer a genero; fratrum quoque gratia rarast.   145
imminet exitio uir coniugis, illa mariti;
lurida terribiles miscent aconita nouercae;
filius ante diem patrios inquirit in annos;
uicta iacet pietas, et uirgo caede madentes,
ultima caelestum, terras Astraea reliquit.   150

The Giants

neue foret terris securior arduus aether,
adfectasse ferunt regnum caeleste Gigantas
altaque congestos struxisse ad sidera montes.
tum pater omnipotens misso perfregit Olympum
155 fulmine et excussit subiecto Pelion Ossae.
obruta mole sua cum corpora dira iacerent,
perfusam multo natorum sanguine Terram
immaduisse ferunt calidumque animasse cruorem
et, ne nulla suae stirpis monimenta manerent,
160 in faciem uertisse hominum. sed et illa propago
contemptrix superum saeuaeque auidissima caedis
et uiolenta fuit: scires e sanguine natos.

Lycaon

quae pater ut summa uidit Saturnius arce
ingemit, et, facto nondum uulgata recenti,
165 foeda Lycaoniae referens conuiuia mensae,
ingentes animo et dignas Ioue concipit iras,
conciliumque uocat; tenuit mora nulla uocatos.
est uia sublimis, caelo manifesta sereno;
l a c t e a nomen habet, candore notabilis ipso.
170 hac iter est superis ad magni tecta Tonantis
regalemque domum. dextra laeuaque deorum
atria nobilium ualuis celebrantur apertis.
plebs habitat diuersa locis; hac parte potentes
caelicolae clarique suos posuere penates.
175 hic locus est quem, si uerbis audacia detur,
haud timeam magni dixisse Palatia caeli.
ergo, ubi marmoreo superi sedere recessu,
celsior ipse loco sceptroque innixus eburno
terrificam capitis concussit terque quaterque
180 caesariem, cum qua terram, mare, sidera mouit.
talibus inde modis ora indignantia soluit:

'non ego pro mundi regno magis anxius illa
tempestate fui qua centum quisque parabat
inicere anguipedum captiuo bracchia caelo:
nam quamquam ferus hostis erat, tamen illud ab uno 185
corpore et ex una pendebat origine bellum.
nunc mihi qua totum Nereus circumsonat orbem
perdendumst mortale genus—per flumina iuro
infera, sub terras Stygio labentia luco.
cuncta prius temptanda, sed immedicabile corpus   190
ense recidendumst ne pars sincera trahatur.
sunt mihi semidei, sunt rustica numina, Nymphae
Faunique Satyrique et monticolae Siluani;
quos, quoniam caeli nondum dignamur honore,
quas dedimus certe terras habitare sinamus.   195
an satis, o superi, tutos fore creditis illos
cum mihi, qui fulmen, qui uos habeoque regoque,
struxerit insidias notus feritate Lycaon?'
    confremuere omnes, studiisque ardentibus ausum
talia deposcunt. sic, cum manus impia saeuit   200
sanguine Caesareo Romanum exstinguere nomen,
attonitum tantae subito terrore ruinae
humanum genus est, totusque perhorruit orbis.
nec tibi grata minus pietas, Auguste, tuorumst
quam fuit illa Ioui; qui postquam uoce manuque   205
murmura compressit tenuere silentia cuncti.
substitit ut clamor pressus grauitate regentis,
Iuppiter hoc iterum sermone silentia rupit:
'ille quidem poenas—curam hanc dimittite—soluit;
quod tamen admissum, quae sit uindicta docebo.   210
contigerat nostras infamia temporis aures;
quam cupiens falsam summo delabor Olympo
et deus humana lustro sub imagine terras.
longa morast quantum noxae sit ubique repertum
enumerare; minor fuit ipsa infamia uero.   215

Maenala transieram, latebris horrenda ferarum,
et cum Cyllene gelidi pineta Lycaei;
Arcados hinc sedes et inhospita tecta tyranni
ingredior, traherent cum sera crepuscula noctem.
220 signa dedi uenisse deum, uulgusque precari
coeperat. inridet primo pia uota Lycaon;
mox ait "experiar deus hic discrimine aperto
an sit mortalis, nec erit dubitabile uerum."
nocte grauem somno necopina perdere morte
225 comparat; haec illi placet experientia ueri.
nec contentus eost: missi de gente Molossa
obsidis unius iugulum mucrone resoluit,
atque ita semineces partim feruentibus artus
mollit aquis, partim subiecto torruit igni.
230 quod simul imposuit mensis, ego uindice flamma
in domino dignos euerti tecta penates.
territus ipse fugit, nactusque silentia ruris
exululat frustraque loqui conatur. ab ipso
colligit os rabiem, solitaeque cupidine caedis
235 uertitur in pecudes et nunc quoque sanguine gaudet.
in uillos abeunt uestes, in crura lacerti;
fit lupus et ueteris seruat uestigia formae.
canities eademst, eadem uiolentia uultus,
idem oculi lurent, eadem feritatis imagost.
240 occidit una domus, sed non domus una perire
digna fuit: qua terra patet fera regnat Erinys;
in facinus iurasse putes. dent ocius omnes
quas meruere pati—sic stat sententia—poenas.'
dicta Iouis pars uoce probant stimulosque frementi
245 adiciunt, alii partes adsensibus implent.
est tamen humani generis iactura dolori
omnibus, et quae sit terrae mortalibus orbae
forma futura rogant, quis sit laturus in aras
tura, ferisne paret populandas tradere terras.

talia quaerentes—sibi enim fore cetera curae— 250
rex superum trepidare uetat, subolemque priori
dissimilem populo promittit origine mira.

The Flood

iamque erat in totas sparsurus fulmina terras,
sed timuit ne forte sacer tot ab ignibus aether
conciperet flammas longusque ardesceret axis. 255
esse quoque in fatis reminiscitur adfore tempus
quo mare, quo tellus correptaque regia caeli
ardeat, et mundi moles operosa laboret.
tela reponuntur manibus fabricata Cyclopum;
poena placet diuersa—genus mortale sub undis 260
perdere et ex omni nimbos demittere caelo.
protinus Aeoliis Aquilonem claudit in antris
et quaecumque fugant inductas flamina nubes,
emittitque Notum. madidis Notus euolat alis,
terribilem picea tectus caligine uultum; 265
barba grauis nimbis, canis fluit unda capillis,
fronte sedent nebulae, rorant pennaeque sinusque.
utque manu late pendentia nubila pressit,
fit fragor: hinc densi funduntur ab aethere nimbi.
nuntia Iunonis, uarios induta colores, 270
concipit Iris aquas alimentaque nubibus adfert.
sternuntur segetes et deplorata coloni
uota iacent, longique labor perit inritus anni.
nec caelo contenta suost Iouis ira, sed illum
caeruleus frater iuuat auxiliaribus undis. 275
conuocat hic amnes; qui postquam tecta tyranni
intrauere sui, 'non est hortamine longo
nunc' ait 'utendum. uires effundite uestras—
sic opus est—aperite domos ac mole remota
fluminibus uestris totas immittite habenas.' 280
iusserat: hi redeunt ac fontibus ora relaxant

et defrenato uoluuntur in aequora cursu.
ipse tridente suo terram percussit: at illa
intremuit, motuque uias patefecit aquarum.
285 exspatiata ruunt per apertos flumina campos,
cumque satis arbusta simul pecudesque uirosque
tectaque cumque suis rapiunt penetralia sacris.
siqua domus mansit potuitque resistere tanto
indeiecta malo, culmen tamen altior huius
290 unda tegit, pressaeque latent sub gurgite turres.
        iamque mare et tellus nullum discrimen habebant;
omnia pontus erat, derant quoque litora ponto.
occupat hic collem, cumba sedet alter adunca
et ducit remos illic ubi nuper ararat.
295 ille supra segetes aut mersae culmina uillae
nauigat, hic summa piscem deprendit in ulmo.
figitur in uiridi, si fors tulit, ancora prato,
aut subiecta terunt curuae uineta carinae;
et modo qua graciles gramen carpsere capellae,
300 nunc ibi deformes ponunt sua corpora phocae.
mirantur sub aqua lucos urbesque domosque
Nereides, siluasque tenent delphines et altis
incursant ramis agitataque robora pulsant.
nat lupus inter oues, fuluos uehit unda leones,
305 unda uehit tigres; nec uires fulminis apro,
crura nec ablato prosunt uelocia ceruo;
quaesitisque diu terris ubi sistere possit,
in mare lassatis uolucris uaga decidit alis.
obruerat tumulos immensa licentia ponti,
310 pulsabantque noui montana cacumina fluctus.
maxima pars unda rapitur: quibus unda pepercit,
illos longa domant inopi ieiunia uictu.

Deucalion and Pyrrha

separat Aonios Oetaeis Phocis ab aruis,
terra ferax dum terra fuit, sed tempore in illo
pars maris et latus subitarum campus aquarum.   315
mons ibi uerticibus petit arduus astra duobus,
nomine Parnasos, superantque cacumina nubes.
hic ubi Deucalion—nam cetera texerat aequor—
cum consorte tori parua rate uectus adhaesit,
Corycidas nymphas et numina montis adorant   320
fatidicamque Themin, quae tunc oracla tenebat.
non illo melior quisquam nec amantior aequi
uir fuit, aut illa metuentior ulla deorum.
Iuppiter, ut liquidis stagnare paludibus orbem
et superesse uirum de tot modo milibus unum   325
et superesse uidet de tot modo milibus unam,
innocuos ambo, cultores numinis ambo,
nubila disiecit, nimbisque Aquilone remotis
et caelo terras ostendit et aethera terris.
nec maris ira manet, positoque tricuspide telo   330
mulcet aquas rector pelagi, supraque profundum
exstantem atque umeros innato murice tectum
caeruleum Tritona uocat, conchaeque sonanti
inspirare iubet fluctusque et flumina signo
iam reuocare dato. caua bucina sumitur illi,   335
tortilis in latum quae turbine crescit ab imo;
bucina quae, medio concepit ubi aera ponto,
litora uoce replet sub utroque iacentia Phoebo.
tum quoque, ut ora dei madida rorantia barba
contigit et cecinit iussos inflata receptus,   340
omnibus auditast telluris et aequoris undis,
et quibus est undis audita, coercuit omnes.
iam mare litus habet, plenos capit alueus amnes,
flumina subsidunt, collesque exire uidentur;
surgit humus, crescunt sola decrescentibus undis: 345

postque diem longam nudata cacumina siluae
ostendunt, limumque tenent in fronde relictum.
redditus orbis erat. quem postquam uidit inanem
et desolatas agere alta silentia terras,
350 Deucalion lacrimis ita Pyrrham adfatur obortis:
'o soror, o coniunx, o femina sola superstes,
quam commune mihi genus et patruelis origo,
deinde torus iunxit, nunc ipsa pericula iungunt,
terrarum, quascumque uident occasus et ortus,
355 nos duo turba sumus; possedit cetera pontus.
haec quoque adhuc uitae non est fiducia nostrae
certa satis. terrent etiamnunc nubila mentem.
quis tibi, si sine me fatis erepta fuisses,
nunc animus, miseranda, foret? quo sola timorem
360 ferre modo posses? quo consolante doleres?
namque ego, crede mihi, si te quoque pontus haberet,
te sequerer, coniunx, et me quoque pontus haberet.
o utinam possim populos reparare paternis
artibus, atque animas formatae infundere terrae.
365 nunc genus in nobis restat mortale duobus—
sic uisum superis—hominumque exempla manemus.'
dixerat, et flebant. placuit caeleste precari
numen et auxilium per sacras quaerere sortes.
nulla morast. adeunt pariter Cephisidas undas,
370 ut nondum liquidas, sic iam uada nota secantes.
inde ubi libatos inrorauere liquores
uestibus et capiti, flectunt uestigia sanctae
ad delubra deae, quorum fastigia turpi
pallebant musco stabantque sine ignibus arae.
375 ut templi tetigere gradus, procumbit uterque
pronus humi gelidoque pauens dedit oscula saxo;
atque ita 'si precibus' dixerunt 'numina iustis
uicta remollescunt, si flectitur ira deorum,
dic, Themi, qua generis damnum reparabile nostri

arte sit et mersis fer opem, mitissima, rebus.'   380
mota deast sortemque dedit: 'discedite templo
et uelate caput cinctasque resoluite uestes
ossaque post tergum magnae iactate parentis.'
obstipuere diu; rumpitque silentia uoce
Pyrrha prior iussisque deae parere recusat,   385
detque sibi ueniam pauido rogat ore, pauetque
laedere iactatis maternas ossibus umbras.
interea repetunt caecisque obscura latebris
uerba datae sortis secum inter seque uolutant.
inde Promethides placidis Epimethida dictis   390
mulcet, et 'aut fallax' ait 'est sollertia nobis
aut pia sunt nullumque nefas oracula suadent.
magna parens terrast. lapides in corpore terrae
ossa reor dici. iacere hos post terga iubemur.'
coniugis augurio quamquam Titania motast,   395
spes tamen in dubiost; adeo caelestibus ambo
diffidunt monitis. sed quid temptare nocebit?
discedunt uelantque caput tunicasque recingunt
et iussos lapides sua post uestigia mittunt.
saxa—quis hoc credat nisi sit pro teste uetustas?—   400
ponere duritiem coepere suumque rigorem,
mollirique mora mollitaque ducere formam.
mox, ubi creuerunt naturaque mitior illis
contigit, ut quaedam, sic non manifesta, uideri
forma potest hominis, sed uti de marmore coepta,   405
non exacta satis rudibusque simillima signis.
quae tamen ex illis aliquo pars umida suco
et terrena fuit, uersast in corporis usum;
quod solidumst flectique nequit, mutatur in ossa;
quae modo uena fuit sub eodem nomine mansit: 410
inque breui spatio superorum numine saxa
missa uiri manibus faciem traxere uirorum,
et de femineo reparatast femina iactu.

inde genus durum sumus experiensque laborum,
415 et documenta damus qua simus origine nati.

The Rebirth of Animal Life

cetera diuersis tellus animalia formis
sponte sua peperit, postquam uetus umor ab igne
percaluit solis, caenumque udaeque paludes
intumuere aestu, fecundaque semina rerum,
420 uiuaci nutrita solo ceu matris in aluo,
creuerunt faciemque aliquam cepere morando.
sic, ubi deseruit madidos septemfluus agros
Nilus et antiquo sua flumina reddidit alueo
aetherioque recens exarsit sidere limus,
425 plurima cultores uersis animalia glaebis
inueniunt; et in his quaedam perfecta per ipsum
nascendi spatium, quaedam modo coepta suisque
trunca uident numeris, et eodem in corpore saepe
altera pars uiuit, rudis est pars altera tellus.
430 quippe ubi temperiem sumpsere umorque calorque,
concipiunt, et ab his oriuntur cuncta duobus;
cumque sit ignis aquae pugnax, uapor umidus omnes
res creat et discors concordia fetibus aptast.
ergo, ubi diluuio tellus lutulenta recenti
435 solibus aetheriis altoque recanduit aestu,
edidit innumeras species, partimque figuras
rettulit antiquas, partim noua monstra creauit.

Python

illa quidem nollet sed te quoque, maxime Python,
tum genuit, populisque nouis, incognite serpens,
440 terror eras—tantum spatii de monte tenebas.
hunc deus arquitenens, numquam letalibus armis
ante nisi in dammis capreisque fugacibus usus,
mille grauem telis, exhausta paene pharetra,

perdidit effuso per uulnera nigra ueneno.
neue operis famam possit delere uetustas,   445
instituit sacros celebri certamine ludos,
P y t h i a de domitae serpentis nomine dictos.
hic iuuenum quicumque manu pedibusue rotaue
uicerat, aesculeae capiebat frondis honorem.
nondum laurus erat, longoque decentia crine   450
tempora cingebat de qualibet arbore Phoebus.

Apollo and Daphne

   primus amor Phoebi Daphne Peneia, quem non
fors ignara dedit sed saeua Cupidinis ira.
Delius hunc, nuper uicta serpente superbus,
uiderat adducto flectentem cornua neruo;   455
'quid' que 'tibi, lasciue puer, cum fortibus armis?'
dixerat; 'ista decent umeros gestamina nostros,
qui dare certa ferae, dare uulnera possumus hosti,
qui modo pestifero tot iugera uentre prementem
strauimus innumeris tumidum Pythona sagittis.   460
tu face nescioquos esto contentus amores
inritare tua, nec laudes adsere nostras.'
filius huic Veneris 'figat tuus omnia, Phoebe,
te meus arcus' ait; 'quantoque animalia cedunt
cuncta deo, tanto minor est tua gloria nostra.'   465
dixit, et eliso percussis aere pennis
impiger umbrosa Parnasi constitit arce,
eque sagittifera prompsit duo tela pharetra
diuersorum operum: fugat hoc, facit illud amorem.
quod facit auratumst, et cuspide fulget acuta;   470
quod fugat obtusumst, et habet sub harundine
   plumbum.
hoc deus in nympha Peneide fixit, at illo
laesit Apollineas traiecta per ossa medullas.
protinus alter amat, fugit altera nomen amantis,

475 siluarum latebris captiuarumque ferarum
exuuiis gaudens, innuptaeque aemula Phoebes.
uitta coercebat positos sine lege capillos;
multi illam petiere, illa auersata petentes
impatiens expersque uiri nemora auia lustrat,
480 nec quid Hymen, quid amor, quid sint conubia curat.
saepe pater dixit 'generum mihi, filia, debes';
saepe pater dixit 'debes mihi, nata, nepotes':
illa, uelut crimen taedas exosa iugales,
pulchra uerecundo suffuderat ora ruborem,
485 inque patris blandis haerens ceruice lacertis
'da mihi perpetua, genitor carissime,' dixit,
'uirginitate frui. dedit hoc pater ante Dianae.'
ille quidem obsequitur; sed te decor iste quod optas
esse uetat, uotoque tuo tua forma repugnat.
490 Phoebus amat, uisaeque cupit conubia Daphnes,
quodque cupit sperat, suaque illum oracula fallunt.
utque leues stipulae demptis adolentur aristis,
ut facibus saepes ardent, quas forte uiator
uel nimis admouit uel iam sub luce reliquit,
495 sic deus in flammas abiit, sic pectore toto
uritur, et sterilem sperando nutrit amorem.
spectat inornatos collo pendere capillos,
et 'quid si comantur?' ait; uidet igne micantes,
sideribus similes, oculos; uidet oscula, quae non
500 est uidisse satis; laudat digitosque manusque
bracchiaque et nudos media plus parte lacertos:
siqua latent meliora putat. fugit ocior aura
illa leui, neque ad haec reuocantis uerba resistit:
'nympha, precor, Penei, mane; non insequor hostis:
505 nympha, mane. sic agna lupum, sic cerua leonem,
sic aquilam penna fugiunt trepidante columbae,
hostes quaeque suos. amor est mihi causa sequendi.
me miserum, ne prona cadas indignaue laedi

crura notent sentes et sim tibi causa doloris.
aspera qua properas loca sunt. moderatius, oro,   510
curre fugamque inhibe: moderatius insequar ipse.
cui placeas inquire tamen. non incola montis,
non ego sum pastor, non hic armenta gregesque
horridus obseruo. nescis, temeraria, nescis
quem fugias, ideoque fugis. mihi Delphica tellus   515
et Claros et Tenedos Patareaque regia seruit.
Iuppiter est genitor. per me quod eritque fuitque
estque patet; per me concordant carmina neruis.
certa quidem nostrast, nostra tamen una sagitta
certior, in uacuo quae uulnera pectore fecit.   520
inuentum medicina meumst, opiferque per orbem
dicor, et herbarum subiecta potentia nobis.
ei mihi quod nullis amor est sanabilis herbis
nec prosunt domino quae prosunt omnibus artes.'
plura locuturum timido Peneia cursu   525
fugit, cumque ipso uerba imperfecta reliquit,
tum quoque uisa decens: nudabant corpora uenti
obuiaque aduersas uibrabant flamina uestes
et leuis impulsos retro dabat aura capillos
auctaque forma fugast. sed enim non sustinet ultra   530
perdere blanditias iuuenis deus, utque monebat
ipse Amor, admisso sequitur uestigia passu.
ut canis in uacuo leporem cum Gallicus aruo
uidit, et hic praedam pedibus petit, ille salutem;
alter inhaesuro similis iam iamque tenere   535
sperat et extento stringit uestigia rostro,
alter in ambiguost an sit comprensus et ipsis
morsibus eripitur tangentiaque ora relinquit:
sic deus et uirgost hic spe celer, illa timore.
qui tamen insequitur, pennis adiutus Amoris   540
ocior est requiemque negat tergoque fugacis
imminet et crinem sparsum ceruicibus adflat.

uiribus absumptis expalluit illa, citaeque
uicta labore fugae spectans Peneidas undas
545 'fer, pater,' inquit 'opem, si flumina numen habetis.
546 qua nimium placui mutando perde figuram.'
547 [*uicta labore fugae 'Tellus' ait 'hisce, uel istam*
547a *quae facit ut laedar mutando perde figuram.'*]
uix prece finita torpor grauis occupat artus;
mollia cinguntur tenui praecordia libro;
550 in frondem crines, in ramos bracchia crescunt;
pes modo tam uelox pigris radicibus haeret;
ora cacumen habet; remanet nitor unus in illa.
hanc quoque Phoebus amat, positaque in stipite dextra
sentit adhuc trepidare nouo sub cortice pectus,
555 complexusque suis ramos ut membra lacertis
oscula dat ligno: refugit tamen oscula lignum.
cui deus 'at quoniam coniunx mea non potes esse,
arbor eris certe' dixit 'mea. semper habebunt
te coma, te citharae, te nostrae, laure, pharetrae.
560 tu ducibus Latiis aderis, cum laeta Triumphum
uox canet et uisent longas Capitolia pompas.
postibus Augustis eadem fidissima custos
ante fores stabis, mediamque tuebere quercum.
utque meum intonsis caput est iuuenale capillis,
565 tu quoque perpetuos semper gere frondis honores.'
finierat Paean. factis modo laurea ramis
adnuit, utque caput uisast agitasse cacumen.

The Story of Io

est nemus Haemoniae praerupta quod undique
claudit
silua; uocant Tempe: per quae Peneos ab imo
570 effusus Pindo spumosis uoluitur undis,
deiectuque graui tenues agitantia fumos
nubila conducit, summisque adspergine siluis

impluit, et sonitu plus quam uicina fatigat.
haec domus, haec sedes, haec sunt penetralia magni
amnis; in his, residens facto de cautibus antro,   575
undis iura dabat nymphisque colentibus undas.
conueniunt illuc popularia flumina primum,
nescia gratentur consolenturne parentem—
populifer Sperchios et inrequietus Enipeus
Apidanosque senex lenisque Amphrysos et Aeas;   580
moxque amnes alii qui, qua tulit impetus illos,
in mare deducunt fessas erroribus undas.
Inachus unus abest, imoque reconditus antro
fletibus auget aquas natamque miserrimus Io
luget ut amissam. nescit uitane fruatur   585
an sit apud Manes, sed quam non inuenit usquam
esse putat nusquam atque animo peiora ueretur.
uiderat a patrio redeuntem Iuppiter illam
flumine, et 'o uirgo Ioue digna tuoque beatum
nescioquem factura toro, pete' dixerat 'umbras   590
altorum   nemorum'—et   nemorum   monstrauerat
    umbras—
'dum calet et medio sol est altissimus orbe.
quodsi sola times latebras intrare ferarum,
praeside tuta deo nemorum secreta subibis,
nec de plebe deo sed qui caelestia magna   595
sceptra manu teneo, sed qui uaga fulmina mitto.
ne fuge me—' fugiebat enim. iam pascua Lernae
consitaque arboribus Lyrcea reliquerat arua,
cum deus inducta latas caligine terras
occuluit, tenuitque fugam, rapuitque pudorem.   600
    interea medios Iuno despexit in Argos,
et noctis faciem nebulas fecisse uolucres
sub nitido mirata die, non fluminis illas
esse nec umenti sensit tellure remitti;
atque suus coniunx ubi sit circumspicit, ut quae   605

deprensi totiens iam nosset furta mariti.
quem postquam caelo non repperit, 'aut ego fallor
aut ego laedor' ait, delapsaque ab aethere summo
constitit in terris nebulasque recedere iussit.
610 coniugis aduentum praesenserat inque nitentem
Inachidos uultus mutauerat ille iuuencam;
bos quoque formosast. speciem Saturnia uaccae,
quamquam inuita, probat, nec non et cuius et unde
quoue sit armento, ueri quasi nescia, quaerit.
615 Iuppiter e terra genitam mentitur, ut auctor
desinat inquiri. petit hanc Saturnia munus.
quid faciat? crudele suos addicere amores,
non dare suspectumst. pudor est qui suadeat illinc,
hinc dissuadet amor. uictus pudor esset amore,
620 sed leue si munus sociae generisque torique
uacca negaretur, poterat non uacca uideri.
paelice donata non protinus exuit omnem
diua metum, timuitque Iouem et fuit anxia furti
donec Arestoridae seruandam tradidit Argo.
625   centum luminibus cinctum caput Argus habebat;
inde suis uicibus capiebant bina quietem,
cetera seruabant atque in statione manebant.
constiterat quocumque modo, spectabat ad Io;
ante oculos Io, quamuis auersus, habebat.
630 luce sinit pasci; cum sol tellure sub altast,
claudit et indigno circumdat uincula collo.
frondibus arboreis et amara pascitur herba,
proque toro terrae non semper gramen habenti
incubat infelix, limosaque flumina potat.
635 illa etiam supplex Argo cum bracchia uellet
tendere, non habuit quae bracchia tenderet Argo;
conatoque queri mugitus edidit ore,
pertimuitque sonos propriaque exterrita uocest.
uenit et ad ripas ubi ludere saepe solebat,

Inachidas ripas, nouaque ut conspexit in unda   640
cornua, pertimuit seque exsternata refugit.
Naides ignorant, ignorat et Inachus ipse
quae sit. at illa patrem sequitur, sequiturque sorores,
et patitur tangi seque admirantibus offert.
decerptas senior porrexerat Inachus herbas;   645
illa manus lambit patriisque dat oscula palmis,
nec retinet lacrimas et, si modo uerba sequantur,
oret opem nomenque suum casusque loquatur.
littera pro uerbis quam pes in puluere duxit
corporis indicium mutati triste peregit.   650
'me miserum' exclamat pater Inachus, inque gementis
cornibus et niuea pendens ceruice iuuencae
'me miserum' ingeminat, 'tune es quaesita per omnes
nata mihi terras? tu non inuenta reperta
luctus eras leuior. retices, nec mutua nostris   655
dicta refers; alto tantum suspiria ducis
pectore, quodque unum potes, ad mea uerba remugis.
at tibi ego ignarus thalamos taedasque parabam,
spesque fuit generi mihi prima, secunda nepotum;
de grege nunc tibi uir et de grege natus habendus: 660
nec finire licet tantos mihi morte dolores,
sed nocet esse deum, praeclusaque ianua leti
aeternum nostros luctus extendit in aeuum.'
talia maerentem stellatus submouet Argus,
ereptamque patri diuersa in pascua natam   665
abstrahit. ipse procul montis sublime cacumen
occupat, unde sedens partes speculatur in omnes.
   nec superum rector mala tanta Phoronidos ultra
ferre potest, natumque uocat quem lucida partu
Pleias enixast, letoque det imperat Argum.   670
parua morast alas pedibus uirgamque potenti
somniferam sumpsisse manu tegimenque capillis.
haec ubi disposuit, patria Ioue natus ab arce

desilit in terras. illic tegimenque remouit
675 et posuit pennas; tantummodo uirga retentast.
hac agit, ut pastor, per deuia rura capellas
dum uenit abductas, et structis cantat auenis.
uoce noua captus custos Iunonius 'at tu,
quisquis es, hoc poteras mecum considere saxo'
680 Argus ait, 'neque enim pecori fecundior ullo
herba locost, aptamque uides pastoribus umbram.'
sedit Atlantiades, et euntem multa loquendo
detinuit sermone diem, iunctisque canendo
uincere harundinibus seruantia lumina temptat.
685 ille tamen pugnat molles euincere somnos,
et quamuis sopor est oculorum parte receptus,
parte tamen uigilat. quaerit quoque (namque reperta
fistula nuper erat) qua sit ratione reperta.

Pan and Syrinx: an Interlude

tum deus 'Arcadiae gelidis in montibus' inquit,
690 'inter Hamadryadas celeberrima Nonacrinas
Naias una fuit; Nymphae Syringa uocabant.
non semel et Satyros eluserat illa sequentes
et quoscumque deos umbrosaque silua feraxque
rus habet. Ortygiam studiis ipsaque colebat
695 uirginitate deam: ritu quoque cincta Dianae
falleret et posset credi Latonia, si non
corneus huic arcus, si non foret aureus illi.
sic quoque fallebat. redeuntem colle Lycaeo
Pan uidet hanc, pinuque caput praecinctus acuta
700 talia uerba refert—' restabat uerba referre,
et precibus spretis fugisse per auia nympham
donec harenosi placidum Ladonis ad amnem
uenerit. hic illam, cursum impedientibus undis,
ut se mutarent liquidas orasse sorores;
705 Panaque, cum prensam sibi iam Syringa putaret,

corpore pro nymphae calamos tenuisse palustres;
dumque ibi suspirat, motos in harundine uentos
effecisse sonum tenuem similemque querenti.
arte noua uocisque deum dulcedine captum
'hoc mihi conloquium tecum' dixisse 'manebit.'   710
atque ita, disparibus calamis compagine cerae
inter se iunctis, nomen tenuisse puellae.

The Story of Io concluded

  talia dicturus uidit Cyllenius omnes
succubuisse oculos adopertaque lumina somno.
supprimit extemplo uocem firmatque soporem,   715
languida permulcens medicata lumina uirga.
nec mora; falcato nutantem uulnerat ense
qua collost confine caput, saxoque cruentum
deicit, et maculat praeruptam sanguine rupem.
Arge, iaces, quodque in tot lumina lumen habebas   720
exstinctumst, centumque oculos nox occupat una.
excipit hos uolucrisque suae Saturnia pennis
collocat, et gemmis caudam stellantibus implet.
protinus exarsit nec tempora distulit irae,
horriferamque oculis animoque obiecit Erinyn   725
paelicis Argolicae, stimulosque in pectore caecos
condidit, et profugam per totum exercuit orbem.
ultimus immenso restabas, Nile, labori;
quem simul ac tetigit, positisque in margine ripae
procubuit genibus resupinoque ardua collo   730
quos potuit solos tollens ad sidera uultus
et gemitu et lacrimis et luctisono mugitu
cum Ioue uisa queri finemque orare malorum:
coniugis ille suae complexus colla lacertis,
finiat ut poenas tandem rogat, 'in' que 'futurum   735
pone metus' inquit, 'numquam tibi causa doloris
haec erit;' et Stygias iubet hoc audire paludes.

ut lenita deast, uultus capit illa priores
fitque quod ante fuit. fugiunt e corpore saetae,
740 cornua decrescunt, fit luminis artior orbis,
contrahitur rictus, redeunt umerique manusque,
ungulaque in quinos dilapsa absumitur ungues.
de boue nil superest formae nisi candor in illa;
officioque pedum nymphe contenta duorum
745 erigitur, metuitque loqui ne more iuuencae
mugiat, et timide uerba intermissa retemptat.
nunc dea linigera colitur celeberrima turba.

The First Part of the Story of Phaethon

huic Epaphus magni genitus de semine tandem
creditur esse Iouis, perque urbes iuncta parenti
750 templa tenet. fuit huic animis aequalis et annis
Sole satus Phaethon: quem quondam magna loquentem
nec sibi cedentem Phoeboque parente superbum
non tulit Inachides; 'matri' que ait 'omnia demens
credis, et es tumidus genitoris imagine falsi.'
755 erubuit Phaethon, iramque pudore repressit,
et tulit ad Clymenen Epaphi conuicia matrem;
'quo' que 'magis doleas, genetrix,' ait 'ille ego liber,
ille ferox, tacui. pudet haec opprobria nobis
et dici potuisse et non potuisse refelli.
760 at tu, si modo sum caelesti stirpe creatus,
ede notam tanti generis meque adsere caelo.'
dixit, et implicuit materno bracchia collo,
perque suum Meropisque caput taedasque sororum
traderet orauit ueri sibi signa parentis.
765 ambiguum Clymene precibus Phaethontis an ira
mota magis dicti sibi criminis, utraque caelo
bracchia porrexit, spectansque ad lumina solis
'per iubar hoc' inquit 'radiis insigne coruscis,

nate, tibi iuro, quod nos auditque uidetque,
hoc te, quem spectas, hoc te, qui temperat orbem,   770
Sole·satum. si ficta fero, neget ipse uidendum
se mihi, sitque oculis lux ista nouissima nostris.
nec longus patrios labor est tibi nosse penates;
unde oritur domus est terrae contermina nostrae:
si modo fert animus, gradere, et scitabere ab ipso.'   775
emicat extemplo laetus post talia matris
dicta suae Phaethon et concipit aethera mente,
Aethiopasque suos positosque sub ignibus Indos
sidereis transit, patriosque adit impiger ortus.

EXPLANATORY NOTES

[An asterisk preceding a line-number indicates that the line in question is dealt with also in the Critical Notes.]

The short and business-like prologue is matched by the nine- 1-4
line epilogue at the end of *Met.* 15. Ovid states the theme of his
great poem which is to contain some 250 stories of transforma-
tions, and then plunges straight into a description of the first
metamorphosis of all—the creation of the world out of Chaos.
To help him in his task he invokes not the Muse, daughter of
Memory, as might have been expected, but the gods responsible
for the metamorphoses.

fert animus: 'my mind impels me, the spirit moves me'; cf. 775,
and Lucan 1, 67: 'fert animus causas tantarum expromere
rerum'. This use with a dependent infinitive is a poetic extension
of the idiom found in Sall. *Jug.* 54, 4: 'quo cuiusque animus fert,
eo discedunt.'

formas mutatas in noua corpora: might be translated by the one
word 'transformations,' 'metamorphoses'. Cf. *Tr.* 1, 7, 13:
'carmina mutatas hominum dicentia formas'.—Note the decora-
tive antithesis between 'animus' and 'corpora'.

coeptis: 'enterprise'; cf. Virg. *Georg.* 1, 40: 'audacibus adnue 2
coeptis'. For the neuter participle used as a noun cf. 210
'admissum' and note.

nam uos mutastis et illas: Housman in his lectures pointed out
that 'et' here emphasises 'mutastis' rather than 'illas'. The logical
structure is: 'Inspire me to tell of transformations, for you were
also the cause of them'. For a similar displacement of *et* cf.
Her. 2, 10: 'inuito nunc et amore noces', where it emphasises
'nunc' or 'inuito'. Displacement of *et*='and' is common enough,
but for an unusual example see Hor. *Sat.* 1, 5, 86: 'quattuor hinc
rapimur uiginti et milia'.—For *mutastis*=*mutauistis* cf. 606 note.

adspirate: metaphor from a favouring wind, but the idea of 3
inspiration, the divine *adflatus*, is also present. Latin poets often
compare their poems to ships, e.g. *Fasti* 2, 3: 'uelis, elegi,
maioribus itis'.

perpetuum: 'unbroken, continuous'; of a long poem composed 4
of a multitude of episodes skilfully linked together. Cf. Cic.
Fam. 5, 12, 2: 'perpetuae historiae'.

deducite: carries on the nautical metaphor, for *deducere* can mean 'bring a ship into port'. The word is used of spinning too, and in this sense fits *perpetuum*.

ad mea tempora: the last metamorphosis of all is that by which Venus transforms the soul of Julius Caesar into a star (*Met*. 15, 843 ff.).

5-88 Ovid's fine account of the creation of the world and of man cannot be said to derive exclusively from any one philosophical school; he is not a philosopher-poet like Lucretius and has no thought of using a scientific cosmogony. His description seems to owe most to Stoic teaching, though it omits Stoic technicalities. It probably embodies the popular view of the world's origin current among those educated Romans who were not Epicureans or Sceptics. The four elements can be traced back to Empedocles of Agrigentum. Anaxagoras had held that Reason (*Nous*) created the world by imposing order on Chaos. Plato regarded the stars as divine beings (73). Socrates had seen in man's erect posture a symbol of his superiority over the other animals (84 ff.). The Pythagoreans originated the doctrine of the Five Zones (45 ff.). The Stoics included all these points in their system, which had as a fundamental tenet the identification of God with Nature (21).

The Creation theme seems to have been popular with Alexandrian poets. Apollonius Rhodius briefly describes how Orpheus sang of the origin and early story of the world (*Arg*. 1, 496 ff.); Virgil gives a similar song to Silenus (*Ecl*. 6, 31 ff.) and to Iopas (*Aen*. 1, 740 ff.). Ovid himself treats the same theme briefly in other works, e.g. *A.A*. 2, 467 ff., *Fasti* 1, 103 ff. and 5, 11 ff. His description here can be compared with Manilius 1, 118 ff.

Milton has worked several ideas from Ovid into his account of Chaos in *P.L*. 2 and of the Creation in *P.L*. 7. We know from Johnson's *Life of Milton* that the *Metamorphoses* was one of his favourite books.

For a full discussion of Ovid's use of Stoic teaching see F. E. Robbins, 'The Creation Story in Ovid Met. 1', *Class. Phil*. 8 (1913), p. 401 ff., and P. DeLacy, 'Philosophical Doctrine and Poetic Technique in Ovid,' *Class. Journal*, Dec. 1947, pp. 153 ff.

6   Nature's face had no recognisable features, but was one undifferentiated mass. Cf. *A.A*. 2, 468: 'unaque erat facies sidera, terra, fretum'.

'orþe: Ovid uses a word that suggests that Chaos had a definite shape either because *orbis* was the only one available for the vague *world* of Chaos (*mundus* would imply order), or because the circle is a symbol of infinity. So in *Fasti* 1, 111 Janus (here= Chaos) says 'qui fueram globus et sine imagine moles'.

quem: the antecedent is probably 'uultus' rather than 'orbe'; 7 cf. 770.

dixere: 'men have called'; for this generalising use of the third person plural cf. 121 *subiere*, 152 *ferunt*.

Chaos: probably derived from Gk. χάσκειν 'yawn, gape', and in its original sense='the Void'; cf. in Norse mythology *Ginnunga-gap* 'the great void'. The word first appears in Hesiod *Theogony* 116. Ovid here uses it in the later sense of a formless welter of matter.

rudis: of raw material not yet worked into shape.

indigesta:=disorganised, amorphous. This is the first appearance of the word; perhaps Ovid coined it, cf. 16 *innabilis*, 289 *indeiecta*.

iners: 'idle, useless'; the word is compounded from *in*+*ars*. 8

semina rerum: a Lucretian phrase. Lucretius uses it of the 9 *primordia rerum* or 'atoms' (cf. 1, 54–61). But Ovid probably has the four elements in mind here.

Note the studied symmetry of the lines; by it Ovid achieves a 10-14 fine poetic effect. To emphasise the confusion of Chaos as contrasted with the order and regularity of the created universe, he places five carefully constructed lines in the middle of a series of lines broken up into smaller fragments.

mundo: the universe, with especial reference to the heavens; cf. Cat. 64, 206: 'concussitque micantia sidera mundus'. The Gk. equivalent is κόσμος.

Titan:=Helios, the Sun, whose father was Hyperion. The latter was one of the Titans, who were the sons of Heaven and Earth.—'The greedy touch of common-kissing Titan', *Cymbeline* 3, 4, 163.

Phoebe: one of the daughters of Earth and Heaven, a Titaness. 11 Her name='the bright one'. She is identified with the Moon, and therefore with Diana, by Augustan and Silver Latin poets; cf. Virg. *Georg.* 1, 431: 'uento semper rubet aurea Phoebe'.

reparabat: cf. Hor. *Carm.* 4, 7, 13: 'damna tamen celeres reparant caelestia lunae'.

Cf. *Pan. Mess.* 151: 'nam circumfuso consistit in aere tellus'. 12

ponderibus librata suis: i.e. balanced by her own gravitational 13 forces. 'ponderibus' here='nutibus'; cf. Cic. *N.D.* 2, 98: 'terra...

undique ipsa in sese nutibus suis conglobata' and *De Orat.* 3, 178: 'terra ... sua ui nutuque teneatur'. Although Aristarchus of Samos had advanced a heliocentric hypothesis, it was generally believed in the ancient world that the earth hung motionless at the centre of the universe, and that its balance was due to the continuous pressure of all its parts inwards towards its own centre; see Cic. *N.D.* 2, 115 ff.—'And earth self-balanced on her centre hung', Milton *P.L.* 7, 242.

14   **Amphitrite:** = the ocean. She was daughter of Nereus and wife of Neptune. Cf. Cat. 64, 11: 'illa rudem cursu prima imbuit Amphitriten'. For the spondaic ending cf. 62, 117, 690, 732.

    longo margine: ablative of place where. We should say 'round'; cf. 15, 741: '(amnis) porrigit aequales media tellure lacertos'—'round the land in the middle'.

15   **utque:** we should translate the *-que* as 'but', after the preceding negative; cf. 18, 330 etc.—The *ut* ... *sic* = 'although ... yet'; cf. 370, 404.

16   **instabilis:** on this analogy Ovid coins *innabilis* 'that cannot be swum in', thus giving *instabilis* an added shade of meaning viz. 'unstable' and 'giving no foot-hold'. Such coinages are common in Ovid; cf. 7 n. and 8, 844 'inattenuata'.

17   **nulli:** sc. *elemento*.

19   **calidis ... siccis:** dative, cf. Cat. 62, 64: 'noli pugnare duobus'; or else *cum* can be understood from the next line.

20   **sine pondere habentia pondus:** lit. 'things having weight (fought with things) without weight'. Latin here feels the need for a definite article. For a similar expression cf. Cic. *Orat.* 4: 'in poetis non Homero soli locus est . . . aut Sophocli aut Pindaro, sed horum uel secundis uel etiam infra secundos' (=*uel etiam iis qui infra secundos sunt*).

21-31 Separation of the elements from Chaos. The elements themselves already exist though in a disorganised state. The act of Creation is conceived as the imposition of order on Chaos. The Christian idea of creation out of nothing was foreign to the ancients; it is not to be found even in *Genesis*.

    deus et melior natura: *et* is here explanatory, adding a phrase that defines *deus*. Cf. the Biblical 'even'. *-que* can be used in a similar way; e.g. 170–1 'magni tecta Tonantis/regalemque domum'.

    The Stoic view was that God and the laws of Nature were synonymous, that the Divine Mind permeated every part of

Nature; cf. Sen. *Ben.* 4, 7, 1: 'quid enim aliud est natura quam deus et diuina ratio toti mundo partibusque eius inserta?'

melior compares the nature of the ordered universe with the nature of Chaos; cf. 6 'naturae uultus'.

litem diremit: 'settled this dispute', a legal metaphor; cf. *Fasti* 1, 107: 'ut semel haec rerum secessit lite suarum'.

caelo: here stands for the two elements, ether and air, and in 22 the next line is divided into its component parts—'liquidum caelum, spissum aer'.—Lines with spondees in the first four feet occasionally occur in O. Others in Book 1 are 24, 119, 157, 550, 570, 663. (See J. J. Hartman, *De Ovidio Poeta*, pp. 3 ff.).

liquidum: 'clear, transparent, tenuous'; cf. 67 and Lucr. 6, 205: 23 'liquidi color aureus ignis'.—'And from the thicke and foggie aire he tooke the lightsome skie', Golding.

quae: i.e. the four elements.—**euoluit**=*extraxit, expediuit,* 24 cf. Ter. *Phorm.* 824: 'ego nullo possum remedio me euoluere ex his turbis'.—**caeco**: suggesting darkness and confusion. Cf. Manil. 1, 131: 'caecaque materies caelum perfecit et orbem'.

dissociata locis: cf. 'diuersa locis' in 40. The abl. is one of 25 respect. The phrase is almost equivalent to *dissociata et in locis suis posita.* The line makes a general statement; the details follow in 26–31.

i.e. *ignea et sine pondere uis conuexi caeli emicuit.*—*conuexus* 26 'arched, rounded' can be applied to what is concave or convex; cf. Virg. *Aen.* 4, 451: 'taedet caeli conuexa tueri'.—'sine pondere' here stands for an adj. parallel to 'ignea'; cf. 8, 518: 'ignauo ... et sine sanguine leto'.

elementaque grandia: refers to the large particles, or atoms, 29 of which the heavy elements, water and earth, were composed. Cf. *Fasti* 5, 13: 'pondere terra suo subsedit et aequora traxit.'

pressa:=*depressa.* The simple verb for the compound is 30 frequent in poetry, e.g. 'the lay *Graved* on the stone beneath yon aged thorn', Gray's *Elegy.*

circumfluus: the first appearance of this word in Latin. Cf. Milton *P.L.* 7, 269: 'for as earth, so he the world/Built on circumfluous waters calm, in wide/Crystalline ocean'.

possedit: from *possido* 'take possession of', not *possideo* 'be in 31 possession of'.

orbem: what is the meaning here? The world is not shaped into a globe until 35. Therefore either Ovid is describing the same events from two different points of view, or 'orbem' means something different here from what it does in 35. It seems simplest to suppose that here it=a flat disc which is conceived as floating on the water. For at this stage of the creation the four elements can be thought of as placed in layers one below the other; in the next stage they become concentric spheres, one inside the other.

32-88 Ovid now goes on to deal with the Creation proper, ordering his ideas well. After the formation of the earth into a globe (34–5) he mounts up the scale of the elements as given in 26–31: (i) water—salt and fresh 36–42; (ii) earth—its configuration, vegetation and climate, with a glance at the zones of the sky 43–51; (iii) air and its phenomena 52–66; (iv) ether and the stars 67–71. The mention of the stars leads into a description of the inhabitants of the various elements (72–5), culminating in the creation of Man.

quisquis fuit ille deorum: Ovid's unknown god towers above the conventional deities of the Pantheon that appear later in the poem.

sic: to be taken with 'dispositam', which is *proleptic*, i.e. it *anticipates* the effect produced by the action of the verb; cf. Virg. *Aen.* 1, 69: 'submersas obrue puppes'=*obrue puppes ut submergantur*. So here the sense is: 'When he had divided the mass so as to arrange it thus. . . .'

33　**secuit sectam:** a favourite Ovidian turn for which the technical name is *anadiplosis*, 'reduplication'; cf. *Am.* 3, 6, 44: 'cedere iussit aquam; iussa recessit aqua', and in this book 167, 386, 402.

in membra coegit: 'confined it to its separate parts'. The verb is almost equivalent to *redegit*, which is the reading of all MSS except the Berne Fragment. For this use of *cogere* cf. *Tr.* 3, 7, 10: 'in alternos cogere uerba pedes' and Cic. *De Orat.* 2, 142: 'pollicitus se ius ciuile, quod nunc diffusum et dissipatum esset, in certa genera coacturum et ad artem facilem redacturum.'

34　**ne non aequalis . . .:** i.e. that it might have no part projecting beyond any other, for this would make it impossible for the earth to be in equipoise at the centre of the universe. This is illustrated by the description of the universe in Cic. *N.D.* 2, 116: 'omnes enim partes eius undique medium locum capessentes nituntur aequaliter' 'for all its parts clutching at the centre from every side maintain a uniform pressure.'

35　**speciem . . . in orbis:** for the order cf. 706: 'corpore pro nymphae'.

glomerauit: 'he gathered, massed'. In classical Latin *glomerare* means most usually 'to gather, or collect, into one' 'to mass, pile up'. The Gk. equivalent is συναθροίʒειν. Cf. Virg. *Georg.* 2, 311: 'glomeratque . . . incendia uentus' 'the wind gathers the separate fires into a general blaze.' For a good discussion of the word see W. H. Semple in *C.R.* 60 (1946), pp. 61 ff.

rapidis: combining the ideas of speed and destructiveness 36 (cf. 58–60) as in 14, 764: 'nec excutiant rapidi florentia uenti.'

terrae: dative, 'put shores round the encircled earth' (cf. 631) 37 —'Then, Seas diffus'd; commanding them to roare/With ruffling Winds, and giue the Land a shore', Sandys.

ambitae circumdare: for the pleonasm cf. 153 'congestos struxisse'. 'Verbum omne', says Quintilian (*Inst. Or.* 8, 3, 55), 'quod neque intellectum adiuuat neque ornatum, uitiosum dici potest'. But here the two words together give a better idea of the magnitude of the earth's circumference, and thus of the ocean surrounding it, than 'circumdare' alone would give. Cf. *All's Well* 5, 3, 41: 'The inaudible and noiseless foot of time'.

obliquis: 'winding'; cf.9, 18: 'cursibus obliquis . . . fluentem' 39 and Hor. *Carm.* 2, 3, 11–2: 'quid obliquo laborat/lympha fugax trepidare riuo?'

diuersa locis: lit. 'apart in place', i.e. in different places; cf. 40 25, 173, Virg. *Georg.* 4, 366–7: 'omnia sub magna labentia flumina terra/spectabat diuersa locis', and *Met.* 11,50: 'membra iacent diuersa locis'.

ab ipsa: sc. *terra* from 37.

partim . . . partim:=*alia . . . alia*. As an equivalent of *alii, alia* etc. *partim* is found in prose too, e.g., Cic. *Off.* 2, 72: 'eorum autem ipsorum partim eius modi sunt . . . partim. . . .'

campo: like *aequor* of a level expanse whether of sea or land, 41 cf. 315 and Virg. *Aen.* 10, 214: 'campos salis aere secabant'.

pro ripis litora pulsant: a good rhythmical effect. The correspon- 42 dence of metrical ictus and word accent suggests the regular beat of waves on the shore and makes a restful end to the long sentence.

The Five Zones are also described by Virgil in *Georg.* 1, 45ff. 233 ff., a passage modelled on Eratosthenes' *Hermes,* and by the author of *Panegyricus Messallae* 152 ff. The zones of the earth correspond to those of the sky. The two frigid zones (Arctic and Antarctic), being furthest from the sun, and the torrid zone (Tropics), being nearest to it, were regarded as uninhabitable; the two remaining zones, the northern extending between

the Tropic of Cancer and the Arctic, the southern between the
Tropic of Capricorn and the Antarctic, were so placed in regard
to the sun that they enjoyed a temperate climate.

dextra . . . sinistra parte: on right and left of the fifth, or torrid,
zone. If Ovid uses the words in the technical sense that they had
in Roman augury, then 'south' and 'north' respectively; cf.
Livy 1, 18, 7 (of an augur): 'regiones ab oriente ad occasum
determinauit. dextras ad meridiem partes, laeuas ad septem-
trionem, esse dixit'. When making their observations the augurs
usually faced the east.

46 **quinta:** this contains the sun's path through the sky; the zone
of the earth corresponding to it is that which lies between the
two Tropics (*quae mediast* 49).

47 **onus inclusum:** the earth, enclosed by the sky.

numero: sc. *zonarum.*

distinxit:=*diuisit*; cf. Mela 1, 4: 'terra . . . zonis quinque
distinguitur'.

48 **tellure premuntur:** Haupt took this to mean 'are contained by
the earth', adding that the verb has not the same idea of pressure
as is found in 14, 6: 'fretum gemino . . . litore pressum'. It is
more likely that the meaning is 'are imprinted, marked, traced,
on the earth', and that Ovid is using simple verb for compound
as in 30. Thus the phrase=*telluri imprimuntur.* For a similar use
of *premere* cf. *Her.* 10, 140: 'litteraque articulo pressa tremente
labat', *Fasti* 6, 610: 'aeterna res ea pressa nota' and *ibid.* 1, 355:
'caprum dentes in uite prementem'=*uiti imprimentem.—premere*
is a favourite word of Ovid's and he uses it in a great variety of
ways; compare this passage with 30, 207, and 459 in this book.

50 **inter utrumque:** 'in between', i.e. between the Tropics and the
Arctic and Antarctic circles. For the neuter cf. *Rem. Am.* 809–10:
'aut nulla ebrietas aut tanta sit ut tibi curas/eripiat: si qua est
inter utrumque, nocet'.

*52 **his:** sc. *plagis.*

qui quanto . . . igni: lit. 'which, by how much the weight of
water is lighter than the weight of earth, by so much is heavier
than fire'. Air is heavier than ether in the same proportion as
earth is heavier than water.

54 **illic . . . illic:** as often, the repetition has a different metrical
ictus; so too in English, e.g. Milton *P.L.* 3, 35: 'Blind Thamyris
and blind Maeonides'. Cf. 327, 329 etc.

consistere: 'to settle'. The word is used of taking up residence, esp. of resident aliens; Caes. *B.G.* **7, 3,** 1: 'ciues Romani qui negotiandi causa ibi constiterant'.

Suetonius (*Aug.* 90) reports that Augustus was frightened of 55 thunder and carried around seal-skin as an amulet against being struck by lightning: 'tonitrua et fulgura paulo infirmius expauescebat, ut semper et ubique pellem uituli marini circumferret pro remedio'; for the seal-skin cf. Pliny *N.H.* 2, 146. According to Pliny (*ibid.* 15, 135) Tiberius wore a laurel wreath for the same purpose: 'Tiberium principem tonante caelo coronari ea (sc. lauru) solitum ferunt contra fulminum metus.'

Seneca *N. Q.* 2, 57, 3, gives the difference between *fulgur* and 56 *fulmen* thus: 'eodem autem modo fit fulgur, quod tantum splendet, et fulmen, quod incendit'. The distinction seems to be that between sheet lightning and forked lightning.—It was believed that these were caused by collision of the clouds; *ibid.* 1, 2, 6: 'nubes conlisae mediocriter fulgurationes efficiunt, maiore impetu inpulsae fulmina'.

    habendum . . . permisit: for the construction cf. 74 and 624.   57
    cum: concessive.   59
    diuerso tractu: 'from opposite quarters.'
    lanient: very strong—'rend, tear in pieces'; Cic. *Tusc.* 1, 108: 60 'Magorum mos est non humare corpora suorum nisi a feris sint ante laniata'.
    tantast . . .: the latter half of the verse is a favourite place for such epigrams, cf. 162, 552, etc.
    fratrum: Hesiod (*Theog.* 378) makes them children of the Dawn and Astraeus; so *Met.* 14, 544–5: 'aequor/Astraei turbant et eunt in proelia fratres'.
    Nabataea: O. uses the word loosely fo . its poetical effect. The 61 Nabataeans did not live very far east; they were an Arab people well-known as traders. Their main city was Petra, which lies midway between the Dead Sea and the Gulf of Akaba. Through Petra came caravans with Arabian spices, perfumes and precious stones, on their way to Gaza or Damascus. In 25 B.C. the Nabataeans helped Aelius Gallus in an expedition against Arabia Felix. See Strabo 16, 4, 21, Pliny *N. H.* 6, 144, and *C.A.H.* 10, 247 ff.— 'The morning gray, The Realme of Nabathie', Golding.
    iuga . . .: the Himalayas, or the Hindu Kush.   62
    uesper: so *das Abendland* in German. Cf. *Tr.* 1, 2, 27–8:'nam 63 modo purpureo uires capit Eurus ab ortu,/nunc Zephyrus sero uespere missus adest.'

64 **septemque Triones**: both the Great and the Little Bear were so called. The Latin name = 'the seven ploughing oxen' as Varro explains (*L.L.* **7**, 74): 'triones enim et boues appellantur a bubulcis etiam nunc, maxime cum arant terram . . .'

65 **horrifer**: cf. 725, making one shudder, causing one's hair to stand on end. So of ghastly voices in Lucr. 5, 996: 'horriferis accibant uocibus Orcum'.

Boreas: a fine description in Hesiod's *Works and Days* 504 ff.

66 **assiduis**: with *pluuia* too; so even when the adj. is put with the second noun, e.g. *Tr.* **3**, 12, 5: 'iam uiolam puerique legunt hilaresque puellae'.

madescit: equivaient to a passive, see 378 n.

67 **carentem . . . 68 habentem**: such rhymes are not uncommon in O, cf. 682–3; 5, 115–6: 'dixit . . . fixit', 164–5: 'duorum . . . armentorum'; 6, 198–9: 'meorum . . . duorum', 639–40: 'uidentem . . . petentem'; and many more. Virgil has them too, though more rarely, e.g. *Aen.* 1, 625–6: 'ferebat . . . uolebat'; 2, 124–5: 'canebant . . . uidebant'; 3, 656–7; 10, 804–5.

69 **dissaepserat**: lit. 'had hedged, or fenced, off'; cf. Sen. *Med.* 335: 'bene dissaepti foedera mundi'.

*70 **pressa . . . latuere**: cf. 290.—Ovid seems to imply that the stars were not made but had existed from the beginning, though concealed in the welter of Chaos.

massa: means a lump of any substance in the raw state, and is here applied to Chaos, as in *Fasti* 1, 108: 'inque nouas abiit massa soluta domos'.

71 **efferuescere**: Dryden makes the meaning plain:

'The Stars, no longer overlaid with weight,
Exert their heads from underneath the Mass,
And upward shoot, and kindle as they pass,
And with diffusive Light adorn their Heav'nly place.'

Virgil uses *efferuere* of Etna in eruption, *Georg.* 1, 471: 'quotiens Cyclopum efferuere in agros/uidimus undantem ruptis fornacibus Aetnam'. Cf. 27 *emicuit*.

72 **neu** = *et ne*: a purely poetical use, cf. 151.

foret for *esset*, see 151 n.

animalibus: includes the gods and the stars. Cf. Sen. *Epist.* 113, 17: 'omnia animalia aut rationalia sunt, ut homines, ut di, aut inrationalia, ut ferae, ut pecora', and Cic. *N.D.* 2, 42: 'sidera autem aetherium locum obtinent. . . . necesse est quod animal in eo gignatur, id et sensu acerrimo et mobilitate celerrima esse'.

astra: probably refers to the fixed stars and 'formae deorum' **73** to the planets.

caeleste solum: 'the firmament'; but cf. Shakespeare, *The Merchant of Venice* 5, 1, 58: 'Look, how *the floor of heaven/* Is thick inlaid with patines of bright gold'.

Cf. *A.A.* 2, 470–1: 'silua feras, uolucres aer accepit habendas; / **74-5** in liquida, pisces, delituistis aqua'.

cesserunt: 'were allotted to, fell to'; cf. Livy 31, 46, 16: 'captiua corpora Romanis cessere'.

agitabilis: first and only here in Ovid. Apuleius seems to be next to use the word. One is reminded of *Macbeth* 1, 6:' The air *nimbly* and sweetly recommends itself / Unto our gentle senses'.—Golding translates: 'The suttle ayre to flickring fowles and birds he hath assygnd'.

> 'There wanted yet the master-work, the end **76ff.**
> Of all yet done; a creature who, not prone
> And brute as other creatures, but endued
> With sanctity of reason, might erect
> His stature, and upright with front serene
> Govern the rest, self-knowing. . . .'
>
> Milton *P.L.* 7, 505 ff.

sanctius: 'nobler, more god-like'. The original meaning of *sanctus* is 'established as inviolate'—hence our phrase 'the sanctity of human life'.

his: of course excludes *astra* and *formae deorum.*

capacius: implying that man of himself does not possess mind; he is a vessel able to receive a share of it: cf. Cic. *Off.* 1, 11: 'homo . . . rationis est particeps'.

'Thou madest him to have dominion over the works of thy **77** hands' *Psalm* VIII, 6.

diuino semine: so the Stoic Cleanthes in his great *Hymn to* **78** *Zeus* says ἐκ σοῦ γὰρ γενόμεσθα, θεοῦ μίμημα λαχόντες μοῦνοι 'for of thee were we born, we alone possessing god's image'; and St. Paul quotes to the Athenians on the Areopagus from the Stoic Aratus: 'For we are also his offspring' *Acts* XVII, 28.

opifex: cf. the Platonic δημιουργός, the Artificer who made **79** the physical universe after the pattern of the eternal Forms and wove into it a soul. Here of course 'ille opifex' is the unknown god of line 32. **origo:** so Virgil calls Aeneas 'Romanae stirpis origo' in *Aen.* 12, 166.

recens: 'fresh, newly made', cf. 424: 'recens limus'. **80**

81   **caeli:** refers to the element of ether, or fire, and is said to be the kindred of earth because all four elements were born together out of Chaos.

82   **satus Iapeto:** Prometheus was the son of the Titan Iapetus, cf. Hor. *Carm.* 1, 3, 27: 'audax Iapeti genus'. Pausanias relates that in his time (2nd century A.D.) near a certain village in Phocis there lay two great stones, in colour like clay and with a smell like that of human flesh, which were believed to be the remains of the clay out of which Prometheus moulded the first men and women (10, 4, 4).

83   *Genesis* I, 27: 'So God created man in his own image'.
       effigiem: derived from *effingo*; there is thus a deliberate play on words with *finxit*; cf. 386: 'pauido . . . pauet'.

84   **prona:** contains the two ideas 'downwards' and 'forwards', cf. 376; 10, 652: 'cum carcere pronus uterque / emicat' of two runners starting.

85-6 A good example of theme and two-fold variation (see Henry *Aeneidea* 1, pp. 745 ff.). 'sublime' is expanded into 'caelumque uidere' and then into 'erectos . . . uultus'.
       It was believed that man's erect posture teaches the end for which he was created. The thought occurs often in ancient literature. Cic. *Leg.* 1, 26: 'nam cum ceteras animantes abiecisset' (i.e. Nature) 'ad pastum, solum hominem erexit, ad caelique, quasi cognationis domiciliique pristini, conspectum excitauit', and Seneca plays on the same theme when he asks (*Ep.* 65, 20) 'uetas me caelo interesse, id est iubes me uiuere capite demisso?' Cf. too Xen. *Mem.* 1, 4, 11.

87   **sic**=*itaque* here.
       rudis et sine imagine: echoes *rudis indigestaque* (7). Ovid likes rounding off in this way; so 449 is echoed by 565 at the end of the Daphne story.

88   **ignotas:** sc. *adhuc.*

89-150 The idea that man has degenerated is common to the folk-stories of many nations. Behind all these stories there lies a great truth—the Christian doctrine of the Fall, expressed pictorially, but with profound spiritual insight, in *Genesis* III. The earliest Greek account, if we except such characteristic praises of the past as those of Nestor in *Iliad* 1, 260 ff., is given by Hesiod (*Works and Days* 109-201). He describes the four ages of gold, silver, bronze and iron, but inserts a fifth—that of the Heroes—between the two last, and regards himself as living in the Iron Age. His account is somewhat confused, for the progress of deterioration, suggested by the order of the metals, is not very clearly brought out, and in any case is broken by the appearance of the Heroes—γένος δικαιότερον καὶ ἄρειον —: moreover each race is a fresh creation by Zeus. The next great passage is that of Aratus (3rd cent. B.C.) in his *Phaenomena* 96–136. His narrative is 'a revision of Hesiod under Stoic influence'. He reduces the number of the races to three—gold, silver and bronze—and makes them of one descent. He emphasises the moral regression of man in spite of technical advances. Tibullus (1, 3, 35 ff.) describes two ages, ruled over by Saturn and Jupiter respectively; so too Virgil in *Georgics* 1, 121 ff. In the beautiful lines that follow Ovid skilfully harmonises these variants. He assigns the Golden Age to Saturn's reign, the others to Jupiter's. He keeps the ethical view-point of Aratus. He goes back to Hesiod's five ages, though with a difference; the Iron Age affords him a motive for the introduction of the Flood story, and his fifth age begins with the creation of men and women from stones thrown by Deucalion and Pyrrha. (See Lovejay and Boas, *Documentary History of Primitivism*, and K. F. Smith, *Ages of the World*, in the *Encycl. of Religion and Ethics*.) Other Ovidian descriptions of Saturn's reign can be found in *Am.* 3, 8, 35 ff., *Met.* 15, 96 ff., *Fasti* 2, 289 ff., and cf. Virg. *Ecl.* 4, Hor. *Epod.* 16, Tac. *Ann.* 3, 26, and Homer *Od.* 9, 106 ff.

aetas: if one must be pedantic='generation', as *sata* shows; so Cic. *Sen.* 46: 'conuiuiis delector, nec cum aequalibus solum ... sed cum uestra etiam aetate atque uobiscum'—'men of your generation . . .'

uindice: either 'protector, defender' (9, 241: 'timuere dei pro uindice terrae' i.e. Hercules), or 'avenger' (Cic. *N.D.* 3, 46): 'speculatrices, credo, et uindices facinorum et sceleris' sc. the Eumenides).—For the general sense of this and the next line cf. Virg. *Aen.* 7, 203–4: 'Saturni gentem haud uinclo nec legibus aequam, / sponte sua ueterisque dei se more tenentem'.

fixo aere: the bronze tablets on which laws were engraved and 91 posted up in a public place. So Livy (3, 57) writes: 'leges decemuirales, quibus tabulis duodecim est nomen, in aes incisas in publico proposuerunt'. Cf. too Virg. *Aen.* 6, 622: 'fixit leges pretio atque refixit'.

ligabantur: Magnus takes this to mean that the words were 92 linked together in a connected text, and compares the use of *ligauit* in 25. But surely the words may be said to be 'bound fast' to the bronze tablet because they are indelibly carved into the metal. There seems, too, to be a suggestion of the *binding* nature of the laws, cf. Prop. 4, 4, 82: 'pacta ligat'.—Seneca (*Ep.* 90, 6) quotes Posidonius the Stoic as saying that the need for laws is a sign of human degeneration: 'postquam, subrepentibus uitiis, in tyrannidem regna conuersa sunt, opus esse coepit legibus'.

Dryden has a fine paraphrase of this passage:

'Un-forc'd by Punishment, un-aw'd by fear,
His words were simple and his Soul sincere:
Needless was written Law, where none opprest;
The Law of Man was written in his Breast.'

nec supplex: Golding's version is vivid: 'There was no man would crouch or creepe to Judge with cap in hand'.—Notice how in all this passage O. uses a string of negatives to describe what was NOT going on in the Golden Age, thereby contrasting it with the Iron Age, just as in 10–14 he contrasts Chaos with the ordered universe.

94   **uiseret:** stronger than *uideret*. It can mean to look at attentively, or to visit; cf. Hor. *Carm.* 1, 2, 7–8: 'omne cum Proteus pecus egit altos / uisere montes' and Cic. *Tusc.* 5, 9: 'uisendi causa uenirent, studioseque perspicerent quid ageretur et quo modo'—of spectators at the Games.

96   The impiety of sea-faring is a favourite topic in the Roman poets, e.g. Horace's *Propempticon* to Virgil (*Carm.* 1, 3). Pascal would no doubt have agreed: 'When I have set myself now and then to consider the various distractions of men, the toils and dangers to which they expose themselves in the court or the camp, whence arise so many quarrels and passions, such daring and often such evil exploits etc., I have discovered that all the misfortunes of men arise from one thing only, that they are unable to sit quietly in their own room.'

98   Vegetius thus describes the different wind instruments used for military signalling: 'tuba quae derecta est appellatur; bucina quae in semet aereo circulo flectitur; cornu quod ex uris agrestibus argento nexum, temperatum arte spirituque canentis flatus emittit auditum' *Mil.* 3, 5.

*99   **sine militis usu:** 'without the need of armies'; cf. *Fasti* 2, 500: 'lunaque fulgebat nec facis usus erat'.

securae: originally the English word had the full Latin 100
meaning, e.g. *Judges* VII, 11: 'Gideon . . . . smote the host: for
the host was secure'; and *Hamlet* 1, 5, 61: 'Upon my secure hour'.
—'In firme content /And harmlesse ease, their happy daies were
spent' Sandys.—For other 'golden lines' see 112, 147, 153.

ipsa: 'of her own accord' (strengthened by *per se* in the next 101
line). This is also a prose use e.g. Cic. *Div.* 1, 74: 'ualuae
clausae repagulis subito se ipsae aperuerunt'.

immunis: 'unworked'; the word is explained by the two phrases
that follow—'rastro intacta nec . . . saucia uomeribus:' there
may too be a glance at the meaning 'tax-free'; cf. Livy 21, 45:
'agrum . . . immunem ipsi qui accepisset liberisque.'

rastro: a tool with an iron head equipped with two to four
long and heavy prongs, at right angles to the shaft and spaced
well apart. It was, much more than the spade, the typical
agricultural implement in the ancient world, employed in
breaking up the clods after ploughing and in working and
cleaning the land in vineyards, orchards and gardens. See the
article in Rich.

nullo cogente: Virg. *Georg.* 2, 10–11: 'aliae, nullis hominum 103
cogentibus, ipsae / sponte sua ueniunt'.

arbuteos fetus: still eaten by Italian peasants, according to 104
J. Sargeaunt, *Trees, Shrubs and Plants of Virgil.* Pliny regards it
as poor fare: 'arbutus . . . fructum fert difficilem concoctioni et
stomacho inutilem' *N.H.* 23, 151.

fraga: 'the wild strawberry . . . is abundant in the hilly
districts of Italy and Sicily' (Sargeaunt). Virgil calls them 'humi
nascentia fraga' *Ecl.* 3, 92.

corna: described as 'uictum infelicem' by Achaemenides in 105
Aen. 3, 649. 'The *cornus mascula* grows wild in Sicily, Italy, and
even in Germany, at the present day. Its oblong, red, shining
berries, consisting of little more than a mere membrane covering
a large and hard stone, are sold in the streets of the Italian
towns. "Bad enough food for a hungry man!" said I to myself,
as I spat out some I had bought in Bassano, and tasted for the
sake of Achaemenides' (Henry, *Aeneidea* 2, 505).

duris: 'tough'; cf. *Ex P.* 4, 4, 4: 'mixta fere duris utilis herba
rubis'.—**mora:** = 'blackberries'.

Note that lines 104–5 have a very similar metrical pattern.
Such parallelism is a not uncommon feature of Ovid's style,
esp. in the second half of the line e.g. 194–5, 309–10, 372–3,

527–8. For a more elaborate example cf. 15, 406–7: 'perque leues auras Hyperionis urbe potitus / ante fores sacras Hyperionis aede reponit'.

106   Cf. *A.A.* 2, 622: 'quercus tecta cibumque dabat'. The species of oak referred to is probably that which the Greeks called φηγός, the Valonia oak. Theophrastus describes its fruit as sweetest of all the edible acorns (*H.P.* 3, 8, 2). Identification is complicated by the fact that the Greek for 'sweet chestnut' was Διοσβάλανος = 'Jove's acorn'; see Theophr. *H.P.* 4, 5, 1.

107–   Five of these six beautiful hexameters have their sense
12   complete at the line-ending; this helps to build up the impression of peace and composure.

108   **mulcebant**: 'caressed'; cf. Prop. 4, 7, 60: 'mulcet ubi Elysias aura beata rosas'.

zephyri: the prevailing wind in the Mediterranean spring; cf. *Tr.* 3, 12, 1: 'frigora iam zephyri minuunt'—spring has come to Tomi.

sine semine: 'flowres which without setting grew', Sandys. They were not sown by man; cf. Virg. *Georg.* 1, 22: 'nouas alitis non ullo semine fruges'.

110   **nec renouatus**: =*et non-renouatus*, a use of *nec* common in Latin; cf. Cic. *Tusc.* 1, 15: 'Epicharmus, acutus nec insulsus homo'. *non-renouatus* is here simply a variant of *inarata* in the previous line. For *renouare* of ploughing cf. *Am.* 1, 3, 9: 'nec meus innumeris renouatur campus aratris'.

111   **nectaris**: the tradition was that the rivers ran with wine; e.g. Virg. *Georg.* 1, 132: 'riuis currentia uina repressit'. *nectar* is probably used for 'wine' here; cf. *Georg.* 4, 384: 'liquido ardentem perfundit nectare Vestam'.

112   The liquids and the repetition of *a* and *i* help to make this colourful line sound so well.—Pliny, *N.H.* 11, 8, 18, says that bees make their wax from the flowers of trees and plants; honey, on the other hand, comes out of the air at certain seasons of the year. It drops like morning dew on the leaves of trees, whence the bees collect it (*ibid.* 12, 30). In the Golden Age there was no need for the bees to act as middle-men in this way.

113   Another version has it that Saturn on being driven out by Jupiter fled to Italy and found safe refuge in Latium; see Virg. *Aen.* 8, 319 ff.

114   **sub Ioue**: often used figuratively to mean 'under the open sky'; e.g. Hor. *Carm.* 1, 1, 25: 'manet sub Ioue frigido / uenator', Ov.

Fasti 2, 299: 'sub Ioue durabant'. In its literal meaning here the phrase might well have had for the Roman a suggestion of hardship and inclement weather, and so would lead appropriately enough to the changes for the worse made by Jupiter in the Silver Age.

subiit:=*successit*, cf. 125, 130. The final syllable of this form of the third person singular of the perfect of *eo* and its compounds and of *peto* is long by nature; e.g. 2, 567: 'petiit', 3, 546: 'interiit', 4, 712: 'abiit', 9, 611: 'adiit'.

fuluo: since there were no commas in ancient times, it is a 115 moot point whether this word goes with *auro* or *aere*. Though the adjective is very common with *aurum* (e.g. Virg. *Aen.* 7, 279), its position after the caesura seems to indicate that it goes with *aere* (cf. Lucan 9, 669: 'fuluo . . . aere'). Possibly a Roman would have understood the adjective with both nouns. For a similar case cf. Hor. *Epist.* 1, 14, 43: 'optat ephippia bos, piger optat arare caballus.'

auro:=*aurea prole*; similarly with *aere*. This so-called compendious comparison is the usual Latin idiom; cf. Hor. *Carm.* 3, 6, 46: 'aetas parentum, peior auis, tulit / nos nequiores'.

antiqui: 'ancient' in the sense of 'former'=*pristini*, cf. 423.   116

inaequales: 'variable, inconstant', cf. Hor. *Sat.* 2, 7, 10: 117 'uixit inaequalis clauum ut mutaret in horas'; Sen. *Dial.* 3, 17, 7: 'in totum inaequalis' (ira) 'est: modo ultra quam oportet excurrit, modo citerius debito resistit'.

exegit . . .: lit. 'he made the year pass to its end in four 118 divisions of time through winter, summer...'

Note -*is* at the caesura of this and the two following lines.

canduit: of white dazzling light; cf. Lucan 1, 214: 'cum feruida 120 canduit aestas'.

uentis . . . adstricta: the freezing wind caused the ice to form; cf. 9, 220: 'ferunt imbres gelidis concrescere uentis'.—'Then Icicles hung roping downe', Golding.

domos domus: cf. 141: 'ferrum ferro', 142: 'prodierat prodit'. 121

uinctae cortice uirgae: a sort of brushwood thatching held 122 firm with strips of bark. Seneca, *Epist.* 90, 17, gives a more detailed description of primitive huts: 'non quaelibet uirgea in cratem texuerunt manu, et uili obliuerunt luto? deinde de stipula aliisque siluestribus operuere fastigium, et pluuiis per deuexa labentibus hiemem transiere securi?'

Cf. *Rem. Am.* 173: 'obrue uersata Cerealia semina terra'.   123

124 **gemuere:** 'And oxen under heavy yokes did growne', Sandys. A vivid word perhaps suggesting that the whole creation had now begun to 'groan and travail'; *Romans*, VIII 22: 'scimus enim quod omnis creatura ingemiscit et parturit usque adhuc'.

126 **arma:** since 141–2 seem to imply that neither war nor the mining of metals begin before the Iron Age, Siebelis-Polle interpret *horrida arma* as referring to weapons of stone and wood. It may be supposed that Ovid is thinking of small-scale quarrels, or else that he has slipped into a minor inaccuracy.

promptior = *pronior*.

127 **de:** like *ex*, a regular word to express the material of which anything is made; cf. 575.

128 **uenae:** from meaning a vein or seam of metal ore, *uena* can be applied to a natural bent or disposition; cf. Hor. *A.P.* 409: 'studium sine diuite uena'. One might keep the play on words here by translating 'of baser mettle'.

131 Cf. Virg. *Aen.* 8, 326–7: 'deterior donec paulatim ac decolor aetas / et belli rabies et amor successit habendi'.

134 **ignotis:** either *adhuc ignotis* as not having been sailed on before (cf. 132: 'nec adhuc bene nouerat illos'), or 'unknown' in the sense of 'distant, foreign, remote' (cf. *Tr.* 3, 3, 3: 'in extremis ignoti partibus orbis').

***insultauere:** gives the ships bobbing up and down on the water (thus contrasting with *steterant*) and at the same time implies that it was ὕβρις for men to take to the sea. For the general sense cf. Tib. 1, 3, 37: 'nondum caeruleas pinus contempserat undas'.

135 **auras:** accusative by attraction into the case of *humum*; cf. Ter. *Phorm.* 591: 'ego hominem callidiorem uidi neminem quam Phormionem'.

136 **limite:** Roman surveyors (*mensores*), when making a division of land, first traced out two lines: one, the *cardo* or *limes prorsus* from N to S; the other, the *limes* or *limes decumanus*, from E to W. The land was then divided up into squares by drawing subsidiary *cardines* and *limites* parallel to the principal ones. These *limites* were used as paths, hence the word most often means a field-path or road which at the same time marks the boundary of neighbouring properties. Ovid here uses the word in its technical sense, as does Virgil in *Georg.* 1, 126: 'ne signare quidem aut partiri limite campum / fas erat.'

137 **segetes:** the accusative of the thing may be retained when a

verb that takes two accusatives in the active is used passively, e.g. Hor. *Carm.* 3, 8, 5:'docte sermones utriusque linguae'.

debita: a financial metaphor. Man has an account with the earth: he opens it at seed-time; she pays him back at harvest.

uiscera: Pliny has a similar expression (*N.H*, 2, 63, 157): 138 'penetramus in uiscera (sc. terrae), auri argentique uenas et aeris ac plumbi metalla fodientes'.—Cicero uses *uiscera* of accumulated wealth: *Dom.* 124: 'ad caelum tamen exstruit uillam . . . uisceribus aerarii'; *Q.F.* 1, 3, 7: 'cum de uisceribus tuis et filii tui satisfacturus sis quibus debes'.

> 'By him (i.e. Mammon) first
> Men also and by his suggestion taught
> Ransacked the centre, and with impious hands
> Rifled the bowels of their mother earth
> For treasures better hid'. Milton *P.L.* 1, 684 ff.

recondiderat: the subject is the Earth, to be understood from 139 *terrae* or *humus* in 138.

admouerat: such compound verbs can take a dative in classical prose e.g. Cic. *Tusc.* 2, 61: 'quasi faces ei doloris admouerentur', but where there is real motion it is more usual to find a preposition: Cic. *Rep.* 2, 5: 'ad mare admouit urbem'.

inritamenta malorum: 'incentives to sin'; cf. Livy 30, 11, 7: 140 'inritamentum certaminum equestrium'.

Note the symmetry of the line. 141

utroque: i.e. with iron and gold, on the principle that every 142 man has his price. Cicero *Att.* 1, 16, 12 quotes a saying of Philip of Macedon: 'omnia castella expugnari posse dicebat in quae modo asellus onustus auro posset ascendere'.

Ovid is not so fond of alliteration as Virgil; he has not Virgil's 143 admiration for antiquity. But there are many effective examples in the *Met.*—*crepitantia* can be used of pleasanter sounds, e.g. *Met.* 11, 604: 'inuitat somnos crepitantibus unda lapillis'.

uiuitur ex rapto: cf. Virg. *Aen.* 9, 613: 'comportare iuuat 144 praedas et uiuere rapto'.

socer a genero: a contemporary would think of Pompey and 145 Caesar. Pompey married Caesar's daughter Julia, who was 24 years his junior, in 59 B.C.; she died in childbirth five years later. Cf. Virg. *Aen.* 6, 830–1: 'aggeribus socer Alpinis atque arce Monoeci / descendens, gener aduersis instructus Eois'.

gratia: = *caritas*; cf. Hor. *Epist.* 1, 18, 41-2: 'gratia sic fratrum geminorum Amphionis atque / Zethi dissiluit'.

146 **imminet exitio**: either 'threatens the death of' (cf. Tac. *Hist.* 3, 76: 'Vitellius excidio Tarracinae imminebat'), or 'longs for' (cf. *Am.* 3, 4, 18: 'sic interdictis imminet aeger aquis'). In either case the picture is of someone leaning over and ready to pounce when the right moment comes, cf. 542.

147 Ovid prob. has no particular species of aconite in mind, but uses the word for poison generally. *lurida* will then refer to the effect the poison has on those who drink it, since it gives them a yellowish pallor; cf. Hor. *Epist.* 1, 19, 18: 'exsangue cuminum'. The word usually has sinister associations, e.g. 11, 654: 'luridus, exanimi similis' and Hor. *Carm.* 3, 4, 74: 'luridus Orcus'. For the topic of poisoning see Mayor on Juv. 1, 70.

nouercae: stepmothers had as bad a reputation in the ancient world as they have in the fairy stories; cf. Virg. *Georg.* 2, 128: 'pocula si quando saeuae infecere nouercae', and Tac. *Ann.* 12, 2: 'nouercalia odia'. A contemporary Roman might have thought of Livia, concerning whom ugly rumours circulated (see Tac. *Ann.* 1, 3).

148 **inquirit in annos**: the ref. is to astrology; for a similar construction cf. Tac. *Ann.* 3, 22: 'quaesitumque per Chaldaeos in domum Caesaris'. In a famous sentence Tacitus described astrologers as 'genus hominum potentibus infidum, sperantibus fallax, quod in ciuitate nostra et uetabitur semper et retinebitur' (*Hist.* 1, 22). They possessed considerable influence. Augustus and Tiberius consulted them. It was later made a criminal offence to consult the stars about the fortunes of the imperial house, and for slaves to cast their master's horoscope. See Mayor on Juv. 14, 248.

149 **iacet**: 'lies under foote', Golding. The metaphor here is from the battlefield or the arena.

uirgo . . . Astraea:=Justice, daughter of the Titan Astraeus. As the constellation Virgo she had a place in heaven. As men degenerated after the Golden Age the gods one by one left the earth. Astraea was the last to leave, having lingered among the countryfolk, who preserved the virtues of the Golden Age longest; cf. Virg. *Georg.* 2, 473–4: 'extrema per illos / Iustitia excedens terris uestigia fecit'. Aratus in his *Phaenomena* 127 ff. had said that *Dike* fled to the hills in the Silver Age and left the earth altogether in the Bronze Age.

caede:=*sanguine* as often in the poets; cf. 14, 199: 'uoltus etiamnunc caede madentes'.

The battle of the giants against the gods is not mentioned in 151-
Homer or Hesiod. The latter (*Theog.* 185) merely says that the 62
giants were the offspring of Earth and the blood of Uranus.
Homer (*Od.* 11,305–20) describes how Otus and Ephialtes strove
to place Ossa on Olympus and Pelion on Ossa in order to
climb to heaven. The tradition probably arose from a fusion of
the story of the Titans who fought against the gods with
Homer's account of Otus and Ephialtes. The battle took place
on the plain of Phlegra (Pind. *Nem.* 1, 67), which in ancient times
was identified with various localities, e.g. the promontory of
Pallene, Thessaly and Campania. All these are volcanic areas,
and this suggests that the origin of the tale was some great
eruption or earthquake.—Pope moralises the story thus:
    'Oh sons of earth, attempt ye still to rise,
    By mountains pil'd on mountains, to the skies?
    Heav'n still with laughter the vain toil surveys,
    And buries madmen in the heaps they raise.'
                          Essay on Man 4, 73
and Cicero thus: 'quid est enim aliud gigantum modo bellare
cum dis nisi naturae repugnare' (*Sen.* 5).
    neue: =*et ne*; cf. 72, 445.
    foret: =*esset*; the use occurs in Plautus, the poets and the
historians.
    securior: see 100 n.
    arduus aether: 'regnum caeleste' and 'alta sidera' in the
following lines are variations.
    adfectasse: the verb is used by the historians, of passionate 152
desire or striving for something; Livy 1, 50: 'cui enim non
apparere affectare eum imperium in Latinos?' Cic. only twice
uses it, and then in the phrase from the comedians *iter adfectare*
='to take a road'. *Henry VI*, Pt. 2, 4, 7, 104: 'Have I affected
wealth or honour?'; Pope, *Od.* 11, 386: 'The Gods they challenge
and affect the skies.'
    congestos struxisse: the pleonasm emphasises the height and 153
bulk; cf. 37. 'Go to, let us build us a city, and a tower whose top
may reach unto heaven; and let us make us a name, lest we be
scattered abroad upon the face of the whole earth' *Genesis*
xi, 4.
    The Homeric order of the mountains (*Od.* 11, 315–6) is, from *154-5
below, Olympus-Ossa-Pelion, and Ovid sticks to this elsewhere
(*Am.* 2, 1, 14; *Fasti* 1, 307; *ibid.* 3, 441). But here he appears to give

Ossa-Pelion-Olympus, departing from Homer, as does Virgil *Georg.* 1, 281, and the author of *Aetna* 49.

156   **mole:** of any massive and imposing structure, cf. Hor. *Carm.* 3, 29, 9–10: 'fastidiosam desere copiam et/molem propinquam nubibus arduis'. Here of the three mountains; cf. *Fasti* 5, 41–2: 'fulmina de caeli iaculatus Iuppiter arce / uertit in auctores pondera uasta suos'.

158   **animasse:** 'gave life to, quickened'; *Met.* 4, 619: 'guttae cecidere cruentae / quas humus exceptas uarios animauit in angues'. *anima* is the breath of life. There is thus a slight play in Gray's 'Can storied urn or *animated* bust/Back to its mansion call the fleeting *breath*?'

160   **et illa:** like the men of the Iron Age.

161   **contemptrix:** equivalent to an adjective, cf. Sen. *Ep.* 88, 29: 'fortitudo contemptrix timendorum est'; Luc. 1, 128: 'uictrix causa deis placuit sed uicta Catoni'; Cic. *Tusc.* 5, 5: 'o uitae philosophia dux, o uirtutis indagatrix, expultrixque uitiorum'; Livy 6, 2: 'minime largitor dux': Madvig 60c Obs. 2 ff.

162   **scires:** *Am.* 1, 13, 47 provides one of the pleasantest examples of this potential subjunctive. Ovid, having abused the dawn for arriving so early, ends: 'iurgia finieram. scires audisse—rubebat. /nec tamen adsueto tardius orta dies'.

The ancient Egyptians, according to Plutarch (*Isis and Osiris* 353B) had other views about the Giants' blood: 'They began drinking in the time of Psammetichus; previously they used not to drink wine nor pour it as an acceptable libation to the gods, but they believed it to be the blood of those who had once made war against the gods, and thought that when they were thrown down and mingled with the earth vines sprang up from them.'

164   **facto recenti:** ablative of cause, giving the reason why the story of Lycaon's banquet was 'not yet widely known'.

165   **Lycaoniae:** in O.'s version of the story (211-239), Lycaon, the savage king of Arcadia, was visited by Jupiter disguised as a man. Wishing to test the god, he tried to murder him while he slept. Failing in this, he placed before him at dinner the flesh of a Molossian hostage. Jupiter in his wrath destroyed the house by lightning and transformed Lycaon into a wolf. One tradition has it that the victim was Lycaon's son Nyctimus, another that he was a child taken from the common people, and yet another that the outrage was committed by Lycaon's sons, Lycaon himself being a just king. Frazer sees the origin

of these traditions in the barbarous rites performed in honour of Lycaean Zeus on Mount Lycaeus. It would appear that human flesh was mingled with that of animal victims, and the worshipper who tasted it was thought to turn into a wolf for nine years. Pausanias, writing as late as the 2nd century A.D., hints at the continuance of these rites in his own day. The Greeks saw an etymological connexion between Λυκάων and λύκος 'wolf'.—For a full discussion see Frazer on Apoll. 3, 8, 1, and on Pausanias 8, 2, 1, and 38, 7; for belief in werewolves see *Lycanthropy* in the *Enc. Brit.* It is when talking about werewolves and about these very Lycaean sacrifices that Pliny, with true Roman scorn for the Greek, remarks: 'mirum est quo procedat Graeca credulitas. nullum tam impudens mendacium est ut teste careat' *N. H.* 8, 82.

referens: *refero*=*recordor, memoria repeto,* occurs several times in O., e.g. *Met.* 11, 563: 'illam meminitque refertque'; *Rem. Am.* 299: 'saepe refer tecum sceleratae facta puellae'; *Met.* 15, 27: 'tacitaque recentia mente / uisa refert'. Prop. 1, 1, 38 is another example: 'heu referet quanto uerba dolore mea'.

animo et: aphaeresis of *est* is common in O. at the caesura; 166 cf. 89, 226, 396, 470–1, 530, 537, 539; with other words elision at that point is much rarer, cf. 587, 591, 720, 759. Ehwald remarks that O. only allows himself the elision of a *long* syllable at this point before *et* or *aut,* cf. 2, 314; 5, 670; 7, 639 etc. Ehwald's rule, of course, takes no account of *est.*

conciliumque uocat: an assembly, not a council, which would 167 be *consilium.* After Homer (*Il.* 8, 1 ff; 20, 1 ff; *Od.* 1, 26 ff; 5, 1 ff.) an assembly of the gods became a necessary ingredient of Epic; cf. Virg. *Aen.* 10, 1 ff.—In the following lines O. describes a celestial Rome. Jupiter's headquarters are on the heavenly Palatine; the Milky Way is like the *Sacer Cliuus* leading up to it; the gods are divided into patricians and plebeians; they have their *atria* and *penates.*

est: a favourite starting-point with O. when describing a place; 168 it is usu. followed as here by a dissyllable, cf. 568; 2, 195: 'est locus'; so *Fasti,* 2, 491; 4, 337 etc.

sereno: 'clear, cloudless', often used alone; cf. Livy 37, 3: 'Nursiae sereno satis constabat nimbum ortum'; Sen. *N.Q.* 2, 18: 'quare et sereno tonat?'

nomen habet=*nominatur;* cf. 6, 400: 'Marsya nomen habet', 169 and 15, 96: 'at uetus illa aetas cui fecimus aurea nomen': in the latter the adj. is a quotation and stands outside the grammatical construction of its clause; in English it would be put in quotation marks.

   candore notabilis: the abl. is one of cause, cf. 164 and 198 n.

170   **hac:** abl. of the road by which.

172   **atria:** Ennius outdoes this local colour with his phrase *cenacula maxima caeli*, 'the vast upper-rooms of heaven'.—The atrium was originally the main room of the primitive Roman house, with a hearth in the centre and a hole in the roof to let the smoke out. Servius on *Aen.* 1, 726, gives the derivation: 'unde et atrium dictum est; atrum enim erat ex fumo'; cf. μέλαθρον. Later the *impluuium*, with the *compluuium* above it, took the place of the hearth; the atrium was used as a reception hall and was decorated with the family *imagines*; Sen. *Dial.* 11, 14, 3: 'uides omnes has imagines quae impleuere Caesarum atrium?' Clients paying their calls were received there; Sen. *Dial.* 10, 14, 4: 'quam multi per refertum clientibus atrium prodire uitabunt?' hence *celebrantur* in our passage. Vitruvius (6, 8, 3) knows of atria 100 ft. in length. In the great houses of Pompeii you pass through the atrium into the peristyle, an open court surrounded by colonnades, with a trim garden and a fountain in the centre.

   ualuis: folding-doors, cf. *Met.* 2, 4: 'argenti bifores radiabant lumine ualuae'.

173   **plebs:** cf. Mart. 8, 50, 3: 'cum plebe deorum'. In *Ibis* 79–80 they are specified: 'uos quoque plebs superum Fauni Satyrique Laresque/fluminaque et nymphae semideumque genus', but as we are told (192–5) that these have not yet qualified for celestial citizenship, Ovid may well have other minor divinities in mind here. The medieval author of a sequence in honour of St. Michael adopts O.'s idea and has *plebs angelica* (Dreves *Analecta Hymnica Med. Aev.* 7, p. 195). And Sir Henry Wotton, in his verses to Elizabeth of Bohemia, writes of the stars 'You common people of the skies . . .'

   diuersa: cf. 40; best taken as nom. here.

   potentes . . .clarique: quite often paired in prose, e.g. Sall. *Cat.* 38: 'clari potentesque fieri'; Livy 23, 4, 7: 'familias claras ac potentes Romanis miscuerat'; Cic. *Planc.* 51: 'uiuo patre suo potentissimo et clarissimo ciue'; *id. Lael.* 42: 'quis clarior in Graecia Themistocle, quis potentior?'

174   **penates:** see *N.D.* 2, 68, for Cic.'s explanation of the word:

'di Penates siue a penu ducto nomine (est enim omne quo uescuntur homines penus) siue ab eo quod penitus insident; ex quo etiam 'penetrales' a poetis uocantur'. It is an Ovidian joke to talk of the gods as having household gods.

audacia: cf. Cic. *Tusc.* **3, 20**: 'poeta ius suum tenuit et dixit 175 audacius'.

Palatia: the Palatine, *ipsa imperii arx* as Tacitus calls it 176 (*Hist.* 3, 70).

> 'This glorious Roofe I would not doubt to call,
> Had I but boldnesse lent mee, Heauen's *White-Hall*.
>
> Sandys.

> 'This Place, as far as Earth with Heav'n may vie,
> I dare to call the Loovre of the Skie.'
>
> Dryden.

dixisse: the perfect, for metrical reasons, often replaces the present infinitive in poetry. Sometimes there is a distinction in meaning, but Virg. *Georg.* 3, 435–6 shows that this is not always the case: 'ne mihi . . . carpere somnos / neu . . . libeat iacuisse per herbas'.

ergo: takes up the story again from 167. This resumptive use 177 is not uncommon; cf. 434.

recessu: an inner room; cf. 14, 260–1: 'perque atria marmore tecta / ad dominam ducunt; pulchro sedet illa recessu'.

Homer's splendid picture of Zeus' nod in *Iliad* 1, 528–30 was 179 famous, and often imitated, e.g. Cat. 64, 204: 'adnuit inuicto -80 caelestum numine rector; / quo motu tellus atque horrida contremuerunt / aequora, concussitque micantia sidera mundus'; Virg. *Aen.* 9, 106: 'adnuit, et totum nutu tremefecit Olympum'; Hor. *Carm.* 3, 1, 8: 'Iouis . . . cuncta supercilio mouentis'.

cum qua: = *simul cum qua*; cf. *Ex P.* 2, 2, 64: (uultus) 'qui secum terras imperiumque mouent'.—Note that Cicero usually writes *quocum* (*quicum*), *quacum, quibuscum*.

inde = *deinde*.   181

indignantia: this, like a musical direction to the performer, points to the tone of the following speech; cf. 454 *superbus*, 485 *blandis*.

magis anxius: sc. *quam nunc*.—For *anxius pro* cf. Pliny *Epist.* 182 4, 21, 4: 'pro salute . . . pro moribus anxius'. In 623 we have *anxius* with the genitive.

centum with *bracchia*; *quisque* with *anguipedum* (= the Giants). 183 Ovid has a fine list of monstrosities in *Tr.* 4, 7:   -4

'quadrupedesque hominis cum pectore pectora iunctos,
    tergeminumque uirum tergeminumque canem,
Sphingaque et Harpyias serpentipedesque Gigantas,
    centimanumque Gyan semibouemque uirum.'

captiuo: either proleptic, or more simply 'beleaguered'.

inicere bracchia: there may be a glance at the legal phrase *inicere manum alicui*, 'to claim as one's own property'; cf. *Her.* 12, 158: 'clamarem "meus est" iniceremque manus'.

185   **nam quamquam**: clearly this did not grate on the Roman ear; cf. *A.A.* 2, 131: 'uirgam nam'; Cic. *Off.* 1, 47: 'non adulescentulorum more ardore quodam amoris'.

    ab uno . . . corpore: sedition was then limited to the Giants; now the whole human race is rebellious.—*corpus* just like our use of 'body' in a political or social connexion. This sense is common in Livy, e.g. 26, 16, 9: 'corpus nullum ciuitatis'.

188   **per flumina iuro**: the oath by the Styx was irrevocable, cf. Virg. *Aen.* 6, 323: 'Stygiamque paludem / di cuius iurare timent et fallere numen', 'by whose divinity the gods are afraid to swear and break their oath'; and Hom. *Il.* 15, 37.

189   **Stygio . . . luco**: cf. *Aen* 6, 154: 'lucos Stygis et regna inuia uiuis/aspicies'.

*190   See Critical Notes.

191   **trahatur**: 'be infected'. It is difficult to find a precise parallel to this use of the word. Auson. *Epist.* 23, 28-9: 'sic pars aegra hominis trahit ad contagia sanum / corpus' is near, and was pointed out to me by R. J. Getty. For the general thought cf. 2, 825: 'late solet immedicabile cancer / serpere et inlaesas uitiatis addere partes'.

192   **semidei**: explained by *rustica numina*, which in turn is particularised in the names that follow.—Ovid is fond of compounds of *semi;* he has *semiadaperta, semianimis, semicremus* 'halfburnt', *semifer, semilacer, semisepultus* and others; cf. 228.

193   The humanist Georgius Sabinus in his *Fabularum Ovidii Interpretatio*, of which an edition was published at Cambridge in 1584, has a delightful description: 'Satyri et Fauni traduntur esse homunculi bicornes, naribus aduncis, corpore piloso, et pedibus caprinis; qui utrum sint animalia an Demones, nihil quod affirmem habeo'.

    Faunique: for the lengthening of **que** at the rise of the foot cf. Virg. *Aen.* 3, 91: 'liminaque laurusque dei'; *Met.* 5, 484: 'sideraque uentique'; 4, 10: 'telasque calathosque'. See Postgate, *Prosodia Latina* pp. 32 ff.

Note the close rhythmical resemblance between the two lines. 194
K. Preston (*Class. Phil.* 1919) sees here 'an ingenious adaptation -5
of the appeal to rally to the defence of the *Socii*, who, though not
endowed with citizenship, are entitled to protection'. For this
theme he points to Cic. *Manil.* 6.

   an: introducing a direct question thus, implies a suppressed alt- 196
ernative. Like *num*, in such cases it always expects the answer No.

   illos like *mihi* (197) and *Lycaon* (198) has strong emphasis
by its position. The keeping back of Lycaon, immediate cause of
Jove's wrath, until the very end of the speech, is a most effective
stroke.

   struxerit: common in prose for plotting or instigating; e.g. 198
Cic. *De Orat.* 2, 208: 'odium in alios', Livy 23, 17 and Sen.
Clem. 1, 9, 2: 'insidias', Tac *Ann.* 4, 10: 'mortem'.

   notus: with the ablative probably by analogy with *clarus,*
and cf. 169: 'candore notabilis'.

   feritate: 'brutality', picks up *ferus* in 185; cf. Cic. *Off.* 3, 32:
'ista in figura hominis feritas et immanitas beluae'.

   confremuere: the place was in an uproar; in fact Ovid's synod 199
of gods is a typical Mediterranean assembly.

   studiisque ardentibus: cf. Cic. *Fin.* 2, 61: 'ardentiore studio'.

   deposcunt: in the sense of demanding someone's punishment; 200
so too in prose, e.g. Cic. *Sest.* 46: 'me unum deposcerent'.

   manus impia: the ref. is not very explicit; it may be to the
conspiracy against Julius Caesar. However, if *saeuit exstinguere*
implies that the conspirators did not succeed in their plot,
then one of several conspiracies against Augustus is meant.
Suetonius (*Aug.* 19) gives a list of them; Pliny in his famous
chapter on the chequered fortunes of Augustus (*N.H.* 7, 147)
has the phrase 'totiens petita insidiis uita'. Seneca too, in an
interesting chapter (*Clem.* 1, 9), records the names of those
who plotted against Augustus. One important conspiracy was
that of Varro Murena, the brother-in-law of Maecena., and
Fannius Caepio in 23 B.C. (*C.A.H.* 10, p. 136); another that of
Egnatius Rufus in 20 B.C. (*C.A.H.* 10, p. 145).

   saeuit: for the historic present in the subordinate clause with
past tense in the main clause cf. Hor. *Sat.* 2, 3, 277: 'Marius cum
praecipitat se, / cerritus fuit'; also in prose, e.g. Cic. *Rosc. Com.*
120: 'cum occiditur Sex. Roscius, ibidem fuerunt'.

   Cf. Cic. *Cat.* 4, 7: 'qui populi Romani nomen exstinguere 201
(conati sunt)'.

*202 The 't's and 'r's in this line are picked up again in 'totusque perhorruit orbis'. Persius *Sat.* 1, 109 calls the letter *r* 'canina littera' because it resembles the snarling of a dog. But here it seems rather to emphasise the shudder of fear and horror.

204 **pietas tuorum**) (*manus impia* (200).

205-8 These lines have been censured as tautologous, but they seem perfectly Ovidian. If one dislikes them, one can hold that they would have been altered, had the *Met.* been revised. But Ovid is fond of saying the same thing in different words, e.g. 89–93, 343–5.

210 **admissum**: neuter participle used as a noun, as *quod* shows. Such nouns are formed on the analogy of *mandatum, praeceptum, promissum* etc. Livy is particularly fond of these formations; see Page on *Aen.* 5, 5.

 uindicta: originally the rod with which the magistrate touched the head of a slave as a sign that he was free; cf. Cic. *Top.* 10: 'neque censu neque uindicta nec testamento liber factus est'. The word then comes to mean 'protection, defence', e.g. Livy 34, 49: 'ciuitas in ipsa uindicta libertatis peritura'; and finally 'punishment, revenge', as here.

211 **infamia temporis**: 'an evil report of the age'.

212 *Genesis* xviii, 21: 'I will go down now, and see whether they have done altogether according to the cry of it, which is come unto me; and if not, I will know.'

214 **longa morast**: 'it would take too long'. Latin idiom uses the indicative in such expressions; cf. Cic. *Tusc.* 1, 116: 'rhetores quos enumerare magnum est' and Nepos *Hann.* 5, 4: 'longum est omnia enumerare proelia'.

215 **minor uero**: cf. *Her.* 16, 143: 'minor est tua gloria uero'.

216 **Maenala**: Maenalus is a mountain towards the SE of Arcadia; Cyllene and Lycaeus are mountains in the extreme NE and the extreme SW respectively. But one must not press a poet's geography, particularly when it results in such a melodious line as 217.

*218 **hinc**=*dehinc*, 'next'; cf. Virg. *Georg.* 3, 101, and 181 n. above.

219 Cf. *Fasti* 5, 163: 'inducent obscura crepuscula noctem'.—In spite of the difference between *trahere* and *ducere* given in Seneca's line (translated from Cleanthes) 'ducunt uolentem fata, nolentem trahunt', the two words are often interchanged: e.g. *animam trahere, ducere; nomen, bellum* etc. Ovid has *suspiria ducere* (1, 656) *trahere* (2, 753); *colorem ducere* (3, 485) *trahere* (2, 236). In this book compare 402 with 412.

signa: possibly refers to his look and bearing. So in the 220 *Aeneid* when Iris is disguised as Beroe, her divinity is shown by her appearance: *Aen.* 5, 647: 'diuini signa decoris / ardentesque notate oculos . . .'

discrimine aperto: 'by a simple test'. For *apertus* 'plain, 222 simple' cf. Cic. *Inv.* 2, 55: 'breuis et aperta et ex opinione hominum descriptio'.

The order of the sentence is this: *experiar discrimine aperto (utrum) hic sit deus an mortalis.* Such complication of the word order is rare in O. and is here perhaps designed to represent Lycaon's excitement; cf. *Tr.* 3, 9, 12: ' "Hospes" ait "nosco Colchide uela uenit" ' 'Our Host' he said, '(I recognise the sails) is coming from Colchis'. A good example of wheels within wheels in a pentameter is *Tr.*1,1, 18: 'siquis qui quid agam forte requirat erit.'

dubitabile: perhaps an Ovidian coinage (cf. 16 n.); at any rate 223 this is the first appearance of the word in Latin literature. O. only uses it once more: 'si uirtus in me dubitabilis esset' *Met.* 13, 21. O. has many adjectives of this type: cf. 49, 75, 190: 'euitabilis' (6, 234), 'forabilis' (12, 170), 'indelebilis' (15, 876), 'lamentabilis' (8, 262), 'optabilis' (9, 759), 'populabilis' (9, 262), 'resonabilis' (3, 358)—to mention only a few.

necopina: another word that O. is the first to use. The prose 224 form is *necopinatus*.

grauem somno: a phrase also found in Livy: 'uino et somno graues' 29, 34. Ancient historians sought to give a poetical colour to their style. Thus Quintilian can describe the historical manner as 'proxima poetis et quodam modo carmen solutum' 10, 1, 31.

experientia ueri: 'method of proving the truth'. *experientia* *225 looks back to *experiar* in 222, *ueri* to *uerum* in 223. The line is spoken with indignation or irony.

Molossa: Molossia was in Epirus and extended along the W. 226 bank of the river Arachthus down to the Gulf of Ambracia. Dodona, the most ancient oracle in Greece and dedicated to Zeus, was in Molossia. Ovid is the only author to record this detail of the Molossian hostage.

unius: hence the indefinite article in the Romance languages; 227 cf. 691, also Cic. *De Or.* 1, 132: 'sicut unus paterfamilias his de rebus loquor'; *Att.* 9, 10, 2: 'me una haec res torquet quod non Pompeium tanquam unus manipularis secutus sim.' It was no doubt common in everyday speech.

resoluit: lit. 'unlooses, opens'. *re-* is not infrequently equivalent to 'un-'. In *Ann.* 6, 48 Tacitus uses 'uenas resoluere' of one intending to bleed himself to death.

228 **atque ita:** cf. 377, 711.

229 **mollit . . .torruit:** such fluctuation between historic pres. and aorist is not uncommon, cf. Virg. *Aen.* 7, 169: 'imperat et solio medius consedit auito'; Ter. *Andr.* 128: 'procedit, sequimur, ad sepulcrum uenimus'; *Met.* 4, 729: 'fluctus/ore uomit. maduere graues aspergine pennae'.

230 **quod:** the neuter has a more horrible effect than *quos* (referring
-1 to *artus*); Ehwald aptly quotes Hygin. *Fab.* 136: 'carnem humanam cum cetera carne commiscuerunt idque in epulo ei apposuerunt'. The order of the main clause is *uindice flamma ego euerti tecta in penates dignos domino* (i.e. 'as guilty as their master').—**in domino dignos:** it is more usu. for a prep. to be separated by a gen. from the word it governs; e.g. 35 n., 99, 130, 170, 182. For a parallel to this passage see *Ex P.* 4, 5, 22: 'de tanto dignis consule rebus aget'. This 'inclusive' order is of course not confined to poetry; cf. Cic. *Phil.* 2, 114: 'non in regnum appetentem sed in regnantem impetum fecerunt'.

simul for *simul ac* is common in prose too.

232 The stages of Lycaon's transformation are now described. First, on trying to speak, he breaks into loud howls. Then he is seized by a ravening thirst to kill and runs amok among the flocks. His clothes turn into shaggy hair, his arms into paws. He is a wolf. The contrast between *exululat* (*ex* in this compound is intensive, cf. *edisco*) and *silentia* is most effective.

233 **frustraque loqui:** according to the ancients the two things that marked men off from the animals were reason and speech, *ratio et oratio*; the Gks could put it in one word—λόγος. So O., when relating the transformation of men into animals, emphasises their loss of speech; cf. 637, 745-6; 2, 483; 3, 201, 229 etc.

ab ipo etc. : lit. 'from himself his mouth gathers a ravening ferocity', i.e. his physical thirst for blood results from the madness in his soul. *colligit=concipit*, e.g. 6, 341 : 'sitim collegit ab aestu'. For the use of the word with *rabies* cf. 9, 212 : 'utque dolor rabiem collegerat omnem'; and Virg. *Aen.* 9, 63-4 : 'collecta fatigat edendi / ex longo rabies'.

*235 **uertitur:** a middle use of the passive;=*se uertit:* cf. Cic. *Fam.* 9, 15, 4: 'cum in mentem uenit, ponor ad scribendum'.

nunc quoque: in his new shape too, just as when he was a man.
Notice the alliteration in the following passage; it helps to 236
underline the meaning.

abeunt: *abire* is frequent in Ovid in the sense of 'to be changed
into, turn into', e.g. 4,657: 'barba comaeque / in siluas abeunt';
14, 499: 'comaeque / in plumas abeunt'; hence *Her.* 15, 83:
'abeunt studia in mores' 'interests determine character'.

canities: the colour of the wolf; cf. 6, 527 and 7, 550: 'cani ... 238
iupi', and the Homeric πολιὸς λύκος, *Iliad* 10, 334.

uultus: Cic. *De Orat.* 3, 221: 'imago animi uultus, indices oculi'.

lurent: Chaucer, *Knight's Tale* 2131-2: 'The cercles of his *239
eyen in his heed, They gloweden betwixe yelow and reed'.

Erinys: here not an avenging spirit, but a Demon of madness 241
goading men into crime, as in 11, 14: 'insanaque regnat Erinys'.
Lucan in 4, 187 calls the civil war 'ciuilis Erinys'.

iurasse: the subject is *homines* or *humanum genus* understood. 242
In prose *coniurasse* would be used; cf. Livy 39, 16, 5: 'cum
quibus in omne flagitium et facinus coniurauit'.

putes: potential, cf. 162: 'scires'. The present or perfect
subjunctive in such cases relates to the present or future and
implies that the idea can be realised or verified. The imperfect
or pluperfect subjunctive relates to the past and implies that
the idea is impossible of verification. The first is called the
Ideal, the second the Unreal, Subjunctive. Here the pres.
subj. is used because Jove's audience could verify his statement
by going to look at the state of the world; in 162 the impf. subj.
is used because such verification is impossible.

The last line rounds off Jupiter's speech by echoing its opening. 243
The echo is strengthened by a sort of chiasmus: 'poenas (curam
hanc dimittite) soluit' answered by 'pati (sic stat sententia)
poenas'. Such pattern is evidence of careful composition.

uoce: i.e. in words. 244

adsensibus: 'by applauding'. *adsensus* is any sound of 245
approval; cf. Tac. *Germ.* 11: 'honoratissimum adsensus genus
est armis laudare' (i.e. by clashing their swords or spears against
their shields).

partes implent: 'play their part'. In prose the phrase is Silver
Latin, e.g. Pliny *Ep.* 10, 3b: 'quas partes impleturum te secundum
susceptam fidem confido'.

The repetition of *-tura* (246), *-tura . . . -turus* (248), *tura* (249) 246
must be intentional. The passage seems to suggest a buzz of -9

voices through which can be caught one often repeated word. For the device cf. *Her.* 10, 145-7: 'has tibi plan*gendo* lugubria pectora lassas / infelix *tendo* trans freta longa manus: / hos tibi qui superant os*tendo* maesta capillos'.

247   Cf. Cic. *Sen.* 77: 'Credo deos immortales sparsisse animos in corpora humana ut essent qui terras tuerentur'.

249   **ferisne paret:** this is not a question about the method by which Jupiter intends to destroy the human race; the gods simply ask whether Jupiter means to leave the world to the ravages of wild beasts when men are no longer there to keep their numbers down. Hence Jupiter's answer: all will be well, for a new race will be created.

250   **sibi enim . . .:** the clause is dependent on a verb of saying implicit in *uetat.* Notice the emphasis on *sibi.*

252   **origine mira:** descriptive ablative going with *subolem*—'of miraculous birth'.

254   **sacer:** as being the home of the gods. For *ab* cf. 417 n.

255   **axis:** strictly the imaginary line which passes through the poles of the earth and sky and round which the universe was thought to revolve. But in verse it is used generally for the sky; cf. *A.A.* 2, 94: 'Icare' clamat 'ubi es quoque sub axe uolas?'—For the adj. *longus* cf. 6, 64: 'longum caelum', and such phrases as 'aequora longa, freta longa'.

256   **in fatis:** the best commentary on this is *Met.* 15, 807 ff. Jupiter tells Venus to pay a visit to the record-office of the Three Sisters. There she will find the fate of Aeneas and his descendants engraved on imperishable adamant:

            'sola insuperabile fatum,
        nata, mouere paras? intres licet ipsa sororum
        tecta trium. cernes illic molimine uasto
        ex aere et solido rerum tabularia ferro . . .
        inuenies illic incisa adamante perenni
        fata tui generis. legi ipse animoque notaui'.

Clearly O. conceives Jupiter here as subordinate to the Fates, whose edicts he may delay or hasten, but can never annul.—For the phrase cf. *Fasti* 1, 481: 'sic erat in fatis'; *Tr.* 3, 2, 1: 'ergo erat in fatis'; Sen. *N.Q.* 2, 37: 'si ipsum quoque in fato est'.

257   **correpta:** sc. *flammis*; the participle should also be understood with *mare* and *tellus.*—Heraclitus held that the world periodically returns to that elemental fire from which it sprang, and is then born again. The Stoics took this doctrine over and

combined it with the Pythagorean conception of the *magnus annus*. A great year is the length of time it takes for the sun, moon and planets to return to their original positions. At the end of each great year, in the Stoic view, came the conflagration. Thereafter the world would be re-created and history would repeat the pattern of the previous great year down to the minutest details. Cf. 2 *Peter* III, 10: 'But the day of the Lord will come as a thief in the night: in the which the heavens shall pass away with a great noise, and the elements shall melt with fervent heat, the earth also and the works that are therein shall be burnt up.'

mundi moles operosa: 'the massive complexity of the universe', *258 cf. Lucr. 5, 96: 'moles et machina mundi', and Sen. *Epigr.* 7, 5: 'moles pulcherrima caeli'.—For *operosus* in the sense of 'highly wrought, costing much labour' cf. 15, 666: 'proceres ad templa petiti / conueniunt operosa dei', and Horace's 'diuitias operosiores' in *Carm.* 3, 1, 48.

laboret: 'should go to wrecke', Golding. The word is quite common in Caesar for 'to be in great danger, to be hard pressed' e.g. *B.G.* 7, 85: 'maxime ad superiores munitiones laboratur' (impersonal passive).

Cyclopum: the Cyclops work in the blast-furnaces of Vulcan, 259 stripped to the waist, forging thunderbolts for Jupiter; see Virgil's fine picture in *Georg.* 4, 170 ff and *Aen.* 8, 424 ff.

nimbos: Henry on *Aen.* 2, 616 has a good definition: '*nimbus* 261 is never *nubes*, but always that combination of darkness, heavy rain (or hail), wind, thunder and lightning called in Germany *Gewitter* and in Italy *temporale*, but for which the English language possesses no more appropriate appellation than *thunder-storm*.' See *Aen.* 2, 113: 'toto sonuerunt aethere nimbi'; 4, 120: 'his ego nigrantem commixta grandine nimbum / ... infundam'.

This whole passage is a masterpiece of Ovidian description. 262- Its structure is worth close examination, for it shows how 312 a rhetorically trained poet set about his work. There are two main divisions, describing (A) how the flood happened (262-90), and (B) what it was like (291-312). (A) is subdivided thus: (i) the rainstorm brought on by Notus (262-71) and the damage it caused (272-3); (ii) the rivers, under Neptune's orders (274-84), and the damage they caused (285-90). (B) is planned thus: (i) general picture of the flood (291-2); (ii) detailed pictures (293-308), showing (a) a surface view—human beings (293-6),

(b) the underwater scene—fishes and Nereids (297-303), (c) surface view again—animals this time (304-8); (iii) a return to the general picture, and summing up (309-12). In the detailed pictures O. with his love of contrast emphasises the incongruity of everything, the complete reversal of the natural order. Seneca (*N.Q.* 3, 27, 13) takes him to task over line 304. 'Non est res satis sobria lasciuire deuorato orbe terrarum', he objects, with Stoic seriousness. But O. had no intention of painting a conventionally tragic flood. He gives us a baroque one of his own: *si qua latent, meliora putat.*

262   **Aeoliis:** in *Od.* 10, 1 ff. Aeolus lives on a floating island which from Homer's description might well be an iceberg. Zeus has appointed him to be steward of the winds 'to calm and to rouse whichever he will'. Later Aeolus was imagined to live on the volcanic island of Lipara just North of Sicily, where he kept the winds imprisoned in a huge cave (see Virg. *Aen.* 1, 52 ff.)

 Aquilonem: the North Wind; in 328 he is released to drive the clouds away and bring clear weather; so Virgil calls him *clarus* in *Georg.* 1, 460.

263   **inductas nubes:** 'the gathered, or louring clouds'. Cf. 599, and Livy 1, 29, 4: 'puluisque ex distantibus locis ortus, uelut nube inducta, omnia impleuerat'.

264   Notus is the South Wind. The word is taken direct from the Gk. νότος whose derivatives are νότιος, νοτερός 'damp, moist, rainy'. *Auster* is the true Latin word for the South Wind, cf. 66; the adjectives are *australis* and *austrinus.*—O. is fond of such personifications. The most extended examples in the *Met.* are 2, 760 ff. Envy; 8, 799 ff. Hunger; 11, 592 ff. Sleep; 12, 39 ff. Fame (with which it is interesting to compare Virg. *Aen.* 4, 173 ff). In spite of the familiarity of this device O.'s picture retains its freshness and vigour.—Golding translates thus:

'And set at large the Southerne wind: who straight with watrie wings
And dreadfull face as blacke as pitch, forth out of prison flings.
His beard hung full of hideous stormes, all dankish was his head,
With water streaming downe his heare on both his shoulders shead.
His ugly forehead wrinckled was with foggie mistes full thicke,
And on his fethers and his brest a stilling dew did sticke.'

265   'If his face was covered with darkness,' the hypercritic might object, 'how could the other details of his features be visible for

the poet to describe? O. has therefore not fully realised the figure he wishes to represent.' The objection can be met by quoting Henry on *Aen.* 9, 251: 'uultum lacrimis atque ora rigabat'; he proves that *uultus* is the looking part of the face, the eyes, as opposed to *ora*, the speaking part, the mouth. Just as the meaning of the word is here narrowed, so in 611 it is extended, being used loosely for the whole body.

sinus:=*uestis.* Cf. Virg. *Aen.* 1, 320: 'nuda genu nodoque 267 sinus collecta fluentis'.

late: with *pendentia,* 'the overhanging bank of cloud'. Cf. 268 Luc. 6, 468: 'umentes late nebulas' which Duff well translates as 'the canopy of watery vapour.'

pressit: *veluti spongiam ebriam,* says Lemaire. *fragor* in the next line results from this compression too.

To me the pause after *fragor* gives a vivid impression of the 269 slight delay that often occurs between the first thunderclap and the descent of the rain, when a storm breaks.

hinc:='then', cf. 218 n.

concipit: it was popularly believed that the rainbow sucked 271 up moisture; e.g. Pl. *Curc.* 1, 2, 39: 'ecce autem bibit arcus. pluet credo hercle hodie'. And so Virgil, when describing the signs of rain, has 'bibit ingens arcus' *Georg.* 1, 380.

sternuntur: 'are laid'. This and the next line form a good 272 example of theme and twofold variation.—**deplorata,** like *inritus,* is predicative; cf. 149 *uicta iacet.*

uota: 'the farmer's prayers'=*sata* 'the crops'; cf. 8, 291: *273 'matura metit fleturi uota coloni'. *spes* is used in the same way, e.g. 15, 113: 'spemque interceperit anni'.

qui postquam: quite often at this point in the line: cf. 205, 348, 276 2,403, 5,133, 7,287 etc.

hortamine: Ovid is fond of such neuter formations. The 277 convenience of the ablative singular or neuter plural at this point in the line is evident: cf. 457; 2,596: 'reuocamina'; 828: 'respiramina'; 3,672: 'curuamine'; 15,200: 'imitamina' etc.

immittite habenas: 'give free rein to'. This metaphor from the 280 race-course is kept up in *fontibus ora relaxant, defrenato, cursu, exspatiata. domos* (279) might be compared to the *carceres,* the stalls from which the chariots started the race, situated in the part of the circus known as the *oppidum; mole remota,* the removal of the barriers, might suggest the throwing open of the *cancelli,* the wooden gates of the *carceres.*

282 **aequora**: 'sea' or 'plains'? There is a similar ambiguity in *Aen.* 12, 524: 'dant sonitum spumosi amnes et in aequora currunt'. To a Roman the word, which simply means 'levels', might have suggested both at once. We can see how this might happen from such an English line as *Antony and Cleopatra*, 1, 1: 'this dotage of our general's / O'erflows the measure' where 'dotage' implies that Antony dotes on Cleopatra and prob. also suggests that he is too old for that sort of thing.

   defrenato: the only example of this word.

   uoluuntur: see 235 n.

284 Subterranean waters gush out.

285 *spatium* can be used of the racetrack; *exspatiari* 'to leave the track', cf. 2, 202, of Phaethon's horses, 'exspatiantur equi'.

   The rhythm of these three lines is excellent. Note the rhyme *cumque satis* and *cumque suis*, and the *polysyndeton*, of which Quintilian says 'acriora facit et instantiora quae dicimus' (*Inst. Or.* 9, 3, 54).

286 **arbusta**: the regular substitute in dactylic verse for the metrically impossible *arbores*. *arboribus* being possible in dactylic verse, *arbustis* has its usual meaning of plantations of trees (see Munro on Lucr. 1, 187).

287 **penetralia**: the shrine in every house sacred to the Penates. It was usually in the *atrium*.

   sacris: statuettes of the Penates.

   suis: a free use of *suus* referring not to the subject of the sentence but emphasising the connexion between the *penetralia* and their *sacra*. Cf. Livy 4, 33: 'suis flammis delete Fidenas'.

289 **indeiecta**: another ἅπαξ λεγόμενον; cf. 16n., 282.

   huius: sc. *domus* and take with *culmen*.

290 **turres**: 'its turrets'. The flood rose so high that it covered not only the roof but the towers as well. Pliny mentions that his Laurentine villa had two *turres* (*Ep.* 2, 17, 12) and Seneca describing Scipio Africanus' villa at Liternum says 'turres in propugnaculum uillae utrimque subrectas' (*Ep.* 86, 4). **pressae sub gurgite**: 'overwhelmed by the swirling tide'. For this use of *pressus* cf. *Am.* 2, 11, 6: 'Argo funestas pressa bibisset aquas'. In prose *deprimere* regularly, *opprimere* and *supprimere* more rarely, are used in the sense of 'to sink', e.g. Cic. *Manil.* 21: 'classis superata atque depressa'; *ib.* 33: 'classis a praedonibus capta atque oppressa est'; Livy 22, 19: 'quattuor naues suppressae'.

In *N.Q.* 3, 27, Seneca remarks of this line and 285: 'dixit ingentia et tantae confusionis imaginem cepit'.

A good example of O's. skill in saying the same thing in differ-*291-2 ent ways. It is not tautology, for each variation shifts the point of view slightly. It is not mere technical virtuosity, but wit, flexible, inventive and lively.

cumba: a small, light boat, rowed by one person.   293

adunca='hooked towards', i.e. curved inwards. There is a good discussion of its precise meaning here by L. J. D. Richardson in *Hermathena* 55, 1940, pp. 90-98. He takes it to mean that the bows of the *cumba* curve up and then inwards.   Allcroft-Stout in their edn. make the good observation that O. uses the word here because, like *uncus*, it is also used of the plough, and thus is given point by *ararat* in the next line. Why it is a suitable epithet for the plough can be seen from Rich's picture under DENS 4.

The spondees and the conflict of ictus and accent vividly 294 convey the rhythmical effort of rowing.

nauigat: in *Her.* 19, 47: ' "iam certe nauigat" inquam / 296 "lentaque dimotis bracchia iactat aquis" ', the word certainly means 'swim', and that may be the meaning here; otherwise O. has no mention of men swimming in his Flood.

hic summa etc.: O. has remembered an amusing detail from Horace's flood in *Carm.* 1, 2, 9: 'piscium et summa genus haesit ulmo' and given it a new twist. Sandys translates: 'This from high Elmes intangled Fishes hales', but Golding sees a different picture: 'Another sits afishing in an elme'. Sandys must be right. Dryden, for some reason, omits the line.

si fors tulit: lit. 'if chance brought it about'='sometimes'. 297 The phrase occurs once more in the *Met.*: 'proximus aut idem, si fors tulit' (11, 751), where it is equivalent to *fortasse*.

Notice the placing of the words to bring out the contrast as 299- strongly as possible.—'ponunt sua corpora' well expresses the 300 ungainliness of seals.

tenent: 'in woods the Delphins keepe', Sandys. It may be 302 that O. is here playing with a proverbial expression, cf. Hor. *A.P.* 30: 'delphinum siluis appingit, fluctibus aprum', and Claud. 18, 355: 'aduectum siluis delphina uidebo'.

incursant: the word is used of Polyphemus blundering about 303 after he had been blinded: 'praetemptatque manu siluas et luminis orbus / rupibus incursat' (*Met.* 14, 189-90).

agitata etc.: 'bump and shake the trunks'; the participle is proleptic, cf. 32 n.

304-5 **uehit unda ... unda uehit** cf. 240, 311.—For the homoeoteleuton cf. *Fasti* 1, 141: 'ora uides Hecates in tres uertentia partes'.

fulmen: often applied to the boar. It suggests the speed and destructiveness of his attack, and perhaps too the flash of his tusks as he strikes; cf. 10, 550: 'fulmen habent acres in aduncis dentibus apri', 8, 289: 'fulmen ab ore uenit', *Fasti* 2, 232: 'fulmineo celeres dissipat ore canes'.

306   **ablato**: sc. *fluctibus*.

308   The line makes one see the tired bird fluttering down into the sea. The effect seems to depend on the placing of *uaga* and the resulting rhythm.

309   **tumulos) (montana cacumina**. For the metrical parallelism of
-10 the second half of these two lines cf. 104-5n.

'And vnknowne surges ayrie Mountaines beat'. Sandys.

311   **maxima pars**: sc. *hominum*, as *illos* shows. Cf. Cic. *Balb.* 21: 'magna pars in iis ciuitatibus'.

312   **inopi uictu**: ablative of cause like *facto recenti* (164). Ehwald compares *Fasti* 6, 373: 'nunc inopes uictus ignauaque fata timentes', but there *uictus* is probably genitive, not accusative pl.

313   **Aonios**: poetical for 'Boeotian'.—**Oetaeis**: poetical for 'Thessalian'. Mt. Oeta is in southern Thessaly, in the district known as Oetaea, west of the Malian Gulf.

314   **tempore in illo**: cf. 411; 2, 668; and 12, 512: 'paruoque in tempore'; *Fasti* 2, 230: 'in misero tempore'; *ibid.* 400: 'in tam praecipiti tempore'.

315   **subitarum**: 'sudden' in the sense that they had formed quickly, cf. *subitarius*.

*317   **Parnasos**: it towers above Delphi. For the truth about its supposed two peaks see Jebb on Soph. *Ant.* 1126.

cacumina nubes: *nubes* is acc. pl. In Augustan times there would have been no ambiguity, for the word would have been spelt *nubis*.

318   **Deucalion**: Stories of a great flood that destroyed the human race except for one or two survivors have been found in the Near East, India, the Malay Peninsula, the Indian Archipelago, Australia, the Pacific Islands and the American continent. They are rare in Europe and rarer still in Africa. Until the 19th century it was thought that such traditions confirmed the

Biblical account of a world-wide Deluge. But it was then found that no geological evidence could be produced in support of this tradition and consequently the story in Genesis was widely discredited. In 1872 George Smith was able to decipher the Babylonian epic of Gilgamesh, written on clay tablets dug up by Layard in 1845 from the library of Sardanapalus at Nineveh; one canto of this tells of the flood hero Uta-Napishtim. In this century other fragments of the flood story have come to light, including one found on the site of Nippur and written in Sumerian before 2000 B.C. These versions proved to be the ultimate origin of the Hebrew account in *Genesis*. Then in 1929 Woolley at Ur and Langdon at Kish during their excavations came to a layer of water-laid clay several feet in thickness and plainly the deposit of a deluge. The Biblical account was vindicated and shown to be the legend of an actual local catastrophe.

As regards the Greek flood story of Deucalion and Pyrrha, it is not altogether clear whether it derives indirectly from the Babylonian or whether it arose independently. The earliest mention of it occurs in Pindar *Ol.* 9, 64-7; Apollodorus (1st century A.D. ?) tells it in full in his *Bibliotheca* (1, 7, 2); the much later version found in the *De Syria Dea* ascribed to Lucian reveals evident traces of Semitic influence, for there Deucalion is made to build an ark and take into it pairs of every kind of animal. Frazer, arguing from the scholiast's remark on *Ol.* 9, 64, that Deucalion and Pyrrha landed, according to Hellanicus, on Mt. Othrys in Thessaly, and from the tradition that Deucalion was king of Phthia, regards the story not as the legend of a local flood but as a local myth. In his view the plain of Thessaly surrounded by the mountains of Ossa, Pelion, Olympus, Pindus and Othrys and resembling the bed of a large lake gave the idea of Deucalion's flood to the early inhabitants of the place.

Curiously enough the detail of the stone-throwing that repopulated the earth has parallels among the Macusis of British Guiana and certain tribes on the Orinoco, who say that the two survivors threw coconuts over their shoulders. Again, in the Lithuanian account the couple are ordered to jump over the bones of the earth nine times, whereupon nine other couples rise from the ground. But such parallels may be due to contact with missionaries.

For a full and fascinating account of the various Flood traditions see Frazer, *Folklore in the Old Testament*, vol. 1, pp. 104 ff; for archaeological evidence from Mesopotamia see H. Peake, *The Flood: New Light on an Old Story*, London, 1930.

319   **adhaesit**: 'ran aground'; cf. Cic. *Fin.* 5, 49: 'ut homines ad earum saxa discendi cupiditate adhaerescerent', and Caes. *B.C.* 1, 28: 'naues quae ad moles Caesaris adhaeserant'. **consorte tori**: cf. 10, 246: 'thalami . . . consorte'. *consors* first occurs in O. in the sense of *coniunx*.

320   **Corycidas nymphas**: to whom the Corycian cave on Mt. Parnassus was dedicated.
        adorant: Pliny (*N.H.* 28, 25) describes the ritual thus: 'in adorando dextram ad osculum referimus totumque corpus circumagimus'. So Apuleius describing the unbelief of Aemilianus (*Apol.* 56) says: 'si fanum aliquod praetereat nefas habet adorandi gratia manum labris admouere'. Cf. *Job* XXXI, 26-7.

321   Themis was the goddess representing law as established by custom. Hesiod (*Theog.* 135) makes her one of the six Titan daughters of Earth and Heaven. Aesch. *Eum.* 2-8 says that the first to hold the oracle at Delphi was Earth, then came Themis, then Phoebe, who bestowed it on Phoebus.

322   These qualities did not save Virgil's Ripheus: 'cadit et Ripheus iustissimus unus / qui fuit in Teucris et seruantissimus aequi; / dis aliter uisum . . .' *Aen.* 2, 426-8.

325-6 Such corresponding lines—'liturgical lines' as E. K. Rand calls them (*Ovid and his Influence* p. 81)—are common in O. Other examples are 361-2, 635-6; 2, 82-3; 3, 611-2; 4, 152-3, 575-6; 5, 369-70, 578-9, 605-6, and many more. Here the device seems to emphasise the unity of Deucalion and Pyrrha and their isolation from the rest of the human race.

327   **ambo . . . ambo**: cf. 353: 'iunxit . . . iungunt'.

328   Cf. 262. —330 Cf. 283. *-que* = 'but', see 15 n.

331   Ovid excels in vivid pictures of this kind. The description probably derives from actual paintings or sculptures of Triton.

332   **murice**: his shoulders were encrusted with *murex*, the shellfish from which the purple dye was extracted; cf. Claud. 10, 150: 'uiuo squalentia murice terga' (also of Triton).

335   **bucina**: a poetical variant for *concha* in 333. It is clear from the description that follows and from pictures that Triton's horn is not curved like the military instrument (see 98 n.), but straight and formed in spiral twists; see Rich.

illi: dative of the agent; cf. 341 *omnibus* and Hor. *Epist.* 1, 19, 3: 'carmina quae scribuntur aquae potoribus'. In classical prose this is rarely found other than with the gerundive and the passive participle.

In his lectures Housman pointed out that there should be no 336 comma after *tortilis*: this avoids giving *bucina* two adjectives, or rather, puts *tortilis* inside the relative clause.

turbine ab imo: 'from the lowest point of the spiral'.

in latum: the neuter of the adjective used as a noun: 'splays out into a bell'.

concepit ubi aera: the perfect here expresses repeated action 337 prior to that in the main clause—'whenever it takes in air . . .'. For the tense cf. Cic. *Tusc.* 2, 54: 'qui restiterunt, discedunt saepissime superiores'; for the verb cf. *Fasti* 6, 705: 'modo dimittit . . . modo concipit auras'.

This passage may have suggested Spenser's line: 'Triton blowing loud his wreathed horne'—*Colin Clout*, 245. Compare too Wordsworth:

> 'So might I, standing on this pleasant lea,
> Have glimpses that would make me less forlorn:
> Have sight of Proteus rising from the sea,
> Or hear old Triton blow his wreathed horn.'

The repeated 'o's in this and the previous line suggest the 338 sound of the horn; but often such repetition has no particular poetic significance, e.g. 395-6.

utroque .. Phoebo: i.e. East and West; cf. *Her.* 9, 16: 'implesti meritis solis utramque domum', *Met.* 15, 829: 'gentes ab utroque iacentes / Oceano'.

iussos: cf. 399. **receptus:** in prose the phrase *receptui canere* 340 would be used.

The repetition in these lines is perhaps meant to emphasise the 343 slowness of the process (346 'postque diem longam'). There is -5 no contrast between *amnes* and *flumina*: the one is a variation of the other, just as *sola* is a variation of *humus*. As usual there is pattern: the first three clauses relate to water, the second three to land.

plenos: though now confined to their usual channels, the rivers are still in spate.

uidentur: not 'seem', but 'are seen'; cf. Virg. *Aen.* 8, 707-8: 'ipsa uidebatur uentis regina uocatis/uela dare'.

diem: 'time'; cf. Hor. *Epist.* 2, 1, 34: 'si meliora dies, ut uina, 346

poemata reddit'. In this sense the word is usually feminine.
nudata: sc. *aquis*; the trees still have their leaves in 347.

For the general picture cf. Lucan 4, 128-9: 'tollere silua comas, stagnis emergere colles / incipiunt, uisoque die durescere ualles'.

348 **redditus**: 'restored to view'; cf. the description of two underground rivers in Pliny *N.H.* 2, 225: 'subeunt terras rursusque redduntur Lycus in Asia, Erasinus in Argolica'.

349 **desolatas**: the idea of solitude and emptiness is somehow emphasised by the spondaic movement and the long vowels.

351 **soror**:=*soror patruelis* 'cousin'; *frater* is also found in this sense. Deucalion was son of Prometheus, Pyrrha daughter of Epimetheus; Prometheus and Epimetheus were brothers. So Hermione, who was both wife and cousin of Orestes, writes: 'uir, precor, uxori, frater succurre sorori' (*Her.* 8, 29).

353 Milton seems to have a reminiscence of this line in *P.L.* 1, 87 ff. 'If thou beest he . . . if he whom mutual league/. . . And hazard in the glorious enterprise./ *Joined with me once, now misery hath joined* / In equal ruin. . . .'

355 **duo turba**: 'We two remain; a Species in a pair', Dryden. Ovid is fond of such turns; e.g. 2, 609: 'duo nunc moriemur in una', 8, 636: 'tota domus duo sunt'—**possedit**: cf. 31 n.

Ovid might be criticised for indulging in word-play at this juncture, but his instinct is sound. Jokes are often made in tight corners, to relieve the tension.

356 i.e. even Deucalion and Pyrrha have as yet little reason to be confident of survival. —*quoque*: 'even', as in 145, 553. *adhuc* . . . *non*' is equivalent to *nondum*. *nostrae* is emphatic, being placed at the end of the line when it might have changed places with *uitae*.

358 **quis . . . animus**: *quis* and *aliquis* are sometimes used as
-9 adjectives instead of *qui* and *aliqui*; e.g. Cic. *Diu.* 1, 95: 'quis rex umquam fuit, quis populus . . .'

fatis erepta: 'snatched from death'; *fatis* is dative. Cf. 538: 'morsibus eripitur', 665: 'ereptamque patri'.

360 **quo consolante**: the main weight of the sentence is in the participial phrase, as often in Greek: 'quis consolaretur te dolentem?'

363 **possim**: one would have expected *possem*, since the wish is impossible of fulfilment, but in poetry there are very rare exceptions to the rule, e.g. Prop. 2, 2, 15: 'hanc utinam faciem

nolit mutare senectus' and *Met.* 5, 344: 'utinam modo dicere possim carmina digna dea'.

It has been shown that *atque* is rarely used before words 364 beginning with a consonant in Roman poetry. The figures for the *Met.* are 92.4 per cent elided examples as against 7.6 per cent unelided; for Virgil 88 per cent elided as against 12 per cent. unelided. For details see M. Platnauer 'Elision of ATQUE in Roman Poetry', *C.Q.* 42, 1948, pp. 91 ff. In this book there are seven elided examples (228, 332, 364, 377, 587, 627, 711) and one unelided (605).

exempla: 'patterns'. The word is sometimes used of an artist's 366 model, cf. Cic. *Inv.* 2, 2 (Zeuxis speaking): 'ut mutum in simulacrum ex animali exemplo ueritas transferatur'. Perhaps there is a double meaning: Deucalion and Pyrrha show what men and women used to be, and also what they ought to be (322-3).

numen: i.e. Themis.   368

Cephisidas: in fact the Cephisus rises at Lilaea some distance 369 North of Delphi, and flows into the Copaic Lake. Vollgraff seems right in thinking that O. means the Castalian spring. There was a traditional connexion between the two, for Pausanias (10, 8, 10) says that on certain days the Lilaeans used to throw cakes into the spring of the Cephisus and that these were supposed to reappear in the Castalia. This will then be an instance of metonymy; cf. Virg. *Georg.* 1, 490, where *Philippi* is used for *Pharsalia*; in Silver Latin these are often interchanged.

pariter = 'together, side by side', cf. Virg. *Aen.* 2, 205 (of the snakes): 'pariterque ad litora tendunt'.

ut . . . sic: cf. 15n.   370

uada: 'cutting its usual channel'. The word does not necessarily mean 'shallows' or 'ford'. Lemaire's definition is good: *uădum*—omnis locus per quem aqua uădit, aut in quo aqua continetur, fons, puteus, fluuius, mare, aut, ut hoc loco, alueus. Cf. Hor. *Epod.* 16, 25: 'simul imis saxa renarint / uadis leuata' 'from the lowest depths'; *Aen.* 5, 158: 'longa sulcant uada salsa carina', where it is equivalent to *maria*; Plin. *N.H.* 31, 39: 'imo illa e uado exsilit uena', of the bottom of a well.

inde libatos etc.: 'having drawn water from there'. Clearly 371 *libare* cannot here mean 'pour out as an offering'; if they had poured a libation with the water they could not have sprinkled it on their clothes.—7, 189-90 gives another construction with *inrorare*: 'ter sumptis flumine crinem / inrorauit aquis'.

372-3 Note the metrical correspondence in the latter half of the lines, the like-sounding words *uestigia, fastigia*, and the contrasting *sanctae . . . turpi*; cf. 309 n.

   flectunt: cf. *flectere cursum, iter* etc.

   fastigia: prob. means 'pediment' rather than 'roof' here.

374   **pallebant**: '*Pallidus* is not "pale" in our sense, but "sallow". The Italians were an olive-complexioned people, and when they turned pale, they did not become white, but yellow', Postgate *Sermo Latinus* p. 29.

376   **pronus**: cf. 84 n.

377   **atque ita**: cf. 228, 711.

378   **remollescunt**: the inchoative form of a verb is sometimes a convenient substitute for a passive, cf. 66 *madescit*.

379   **reparabile**: cf. 223 n. It picks up *reparare* in 363.

380   **mersis rebus**: 'a drowned world'. Ovid wittily forms the phrase on the analogy of *res miserae, lassae, fessae* etc. Contrast Juv. 11, 40: 'aere paterno / ac rebus mersis in uentrem'.—Notice the predominance of 's' and 'm' in the line, suggesting perhaps that the prayer was whispered (cf. *pauens* 376).

381   **mota**: the particular emotion is understood from the context, as, for example, in Virg. *Aen.* 6, 399: 'nullae hic insidiae tales; absiste moueri' and *ib.* 405: 'si te nulla mouet tantae pietatis imago'.

382   **uelate caput**: 'As things sacred are dangerous, and as the head is sacred, there are occasions when it might be harmful to the ritual act which is being performed, or disrespectful to the divinity, to uncover it. And conversely dangerous influences might fall on the sacred head at that particular moment' (*Encyc. of Religion and Ethics*, vol. 6, p. 539a). While sacrificing, Roman priests covered the neck and back of the head with the toga (*uelato capite*). Mohammedans and Jews pray with the head covered.

   cinctas resoluite: = *recingite* (cf. 398). So Dido (*Aen.* 4, 518: 'in ueste recincta') and Medea (*Met.* 7, 182: 'uestes induta recinctas') are ungirdled while performing magic rites. On the former passage Servius remarks 'in sacris nihil solet esse religatum'. 'A peculiarity of magic is its fear of knots: every knot represents a binding, and may therefore carry a counteractive force' (*ibid.* vol. 3, p. 428b). Hence it was that in magic ceremonies the clothing had to be free of all knots and the hair loose.

383   **magnae parentis**: cf. a similar riddling oracle given to Tarquin

and Brutus: 'imperium summum Romae habebit qui uestrum primus, o iuuenes, osculum matri tulerit' (Livy 1, 56).

det: dependent on *rogat.* In prose too the *ut* is sometimes 386 omitted, e.g. Caes. *B.G.* 1, 20: 'consolatus rogat finem orandi faciat'.—For the rhyme between the beginning and the end of the line cf. Virg. *Aen.* 6, 213: 'flebant et cineri ingrato suprema ferebant'.

pauido . . . pauet: a similar turn to anadiplosis (33 n.)

umbras: plural perhaps on the analogy of *manes;* cf. 3, 720: 387 'Actaeonis umbrae'.

The order is: 'interea repetunt uolutantque secum inter seque *388 uerba sortis datae caecis latebris'.—*repetunt* 'they recall', cf. *Tr.*   -9 1, 3, 3: 'cum repeto noctem.'—*secum inter seque*; i.e. silently, and aloud to one another.—*caecis latebris*: refers to the dark place of the oracle, hidden in the interior of the temple.

Promethides lit. 'son of Forethought' as *Epimethida* is 390 'daughter of Afterthought'. There is point in the names here. Epimetheus is called ἁμαρτίνοος (Hes. *Theog.* 511) and ὀψίνοος (Pind. *P.* 5, 27).

aut . . . aut: cf. 607-8. The Romans are rather fond of such 391 alternative propositions, e.g. Livy. *Praef.* 11: 'aut me amor negotii suscepti fallit, aut nulla umquam respublica nec maior nec sanctior fuit'. We should prob. translate the first alternative by 'if . . . not . . .' and make the second the apodosis.

Cf. Plat. *Apol.* 6, οὐ γὰρ δήπου ψεύδεταί γε (*sc.* ὁ θεός).   392

lapides: subject of the inf. clause.   393

augurio: 'interpretation'.—**Titania:** because Iapetus, her 395 grandfather, was one of the Titans (cf. 82).—**mota:** see 381 n.

in dubiost: cf. 12, 522: 'exitus in dubiost'.   396

Cf. 381-2. The almost Homeric repetition is in keeping with 398 the naturalness and simplicity of the story.   -9

iussos: 'as they were ordered'; cf. *A.A.* 1, 16: 'uerberibus iussas praebuit ille manus'; *Tr.* 1, 2, 89: 'iussae me aduertite terrae'.

Cf. *Fasti* 4, 203: 'pro magno teste uetustas creditur'. So 400 Quintilian says that the fables of poets are uetustatis fide tuta' (12, 4), and Cicero writes: 'ipsa sors' ('divination by lot') 'contemnenda non est, si auctoritatem habet uetustatis' *Div.* 1, 34. Whereas moderns look forwards, the ancients looked backwards.

saxa: the story may well have arisen from the resemblance of the Gk. words λᾶας 'a stone' and λαός 'people'; see Apoll. 1,

7, 2. Hom. *Il.* ¼4, 611 glances at this resemblance: λαοὺς δέ λίθους ποίησε Κρονίων. One is reminded of John the Baptist's words: 'for I say unto you, that God is able of these stones to raise up children unto Abraham', *Matt.* III, 9.

401   **duritiem**: a more elevated form than *duritiam*, with a tinge of archaism. In 4, 7⁵1, and *Her.* 4, 85, O. uses the commoner form.—The word is not synonymous with *rigorem*. The difference is that between hardness and stiffness. In the next line the hardness is softened (*molliri*) and the stiffness becomes pliant and takes on shape (*ducere formam*). There is the same contrast in 409 between 'solidum . . . flectique nequit'.

402   **molliri . . . mollita**: cf. 33 n. The 'm's and 'l's in the line reinforce its meaning.

    mora: equivalent to *sensim*, 'gradually'; cf. 421 'morando' and *Ex. P.* 2, 7, 79: 'spes quoque posse mora mitescere principis iram'.

    ducere: cf. 219 n.

403   **naturaque mitior**: cf. 21 *melior natura.*—H. Fränkel has pointed out (*op. cit.* p. 77) how *mitior* here picks up *mitissima* (380), *molliri* echoes *remollescunt* (378), *uersast* and *flecti* (408-9) recall *flectitur* (378). 'By this subtle device O. ties up the yielding mercy of the relenting gods with the yielding and relenting of the elements when the merciful miracle is performed'.

404   **ut quaedam . . .**: 'the outline of a human shape could be seen, yet not distinctly, but as though partially carved out of marble, not rounded off enough and very like rough-hewn images'.

405   **potest**: historic present.—**uti**: O. has chosen a felicitous simile to give an air of plausibility to the incredible.

406   **exacta**: 'perfectly finished', cf. Prop. 3, 1, 8: 'exactus tenui pumice uersus eat'; Quint. 10, 7, 30: 'commentarii (Caesaris) ita sunt exacti ut . . . in memoriam posteritatis uideantur esse compositi'.

408   **corporis**: as often = 'flesh', cf. Cic. *N.D.* 2, 139: 'ossa subiecta corpori'; Phaedr. 3, 7, 5: 'quo cibo fecisti tantum corporis?' *facere corpus* is the Latin for 'to put on weight'; the opposite is *amittere corpus.*

    in usum: 'to serve as', cf. 14, 553: 'spinae mutatur in usum' and Tac. *A.* 15, 44: 'in usum nocturni luminis urerentur' of the Christians burnt alive in the *tunica molesta.*

412   **traxere**: cf. 219 n.

413   **femineo**: Latin often uses an adjective where in English we

should have a genitive. *femineus* is of course specially useful because *feminae* is impossible in this metre. So we find 'nomine in Hectoreo pallida semper eram' *Her.* 1, 14; 'puellares tardat harena pedes' *ibid.* 10, 20; 'matronales erubuere genae' *Fasti* 2, 828; in prose. Cic. *Rep.* 2, 50: 'eminet uis, potestas nomenque regium'. In this book see 104, 148, 363, 369, 387 etc.

On the other hand where we should use an adjective Latin often substitutes a noun with a dependent genitive; e.g. Livy 1, 28, 11: 'auertere omnes ab tanta foeditate spectaculi oculos', 'from such a repulsive sight'; Cic. *N.D.* 2, 98: 'fontium gelidas perennitates', 'cool perennial fountains'; *De Or.* 1, 10: 'quanta in obscuritate rerum (mathematici) uersentur', 'in what obscure researches'.

femina: singular in collective sense; cf. 99 and the use of *miles, eques* etc. in Livy and Tac.

inde: here expresses the consequence, like *hinc*, 'hence'; cf. 414 Livy 1, 32, 2: 'inde et ciuibus otii cupidis et finitimis ciuitatibus facta spes . . .' For the thought cf. Virg. *Georg.* 1, 61-3: 'quo tempore primum / Deucalion uacuum lapides iactauit in orbem / unde homines nati, durum genus' and Lucr. 5, 925-6.

documenta damus: 'we give proof', cf. Cic. *Mil.* 8, 22: 'dederas 415 enim quam contemneres populares insanias iam ab adulescentia documenta maxima.'

diuersis formis: descriptive abl. with *animalia*; 'after their 416 various kinds'.

uetus umor: 'the lingering moisture' left behind when the 417 Flood subsided.—**ab igne:** in prose you would expect the instrumental abl., but even there when the meaning is 'in consequence of' *ab* is sometimes used, e.g. Liv. 2, 14, 3: 'inopi tum urbe ab longinqua obsidione'. The use is frequent in O., cf. *Tr.* 1, 11, 12: 'omnis ab hac cura cura leuata meast' and Owen's note.—O. here makes use of the theory of the origin of animal life propounded by Anaximander. For a similar description of the birth of animals see Lucr. 5, 795 ff.

intumuere: suggests the bubbling up of the mud, and also 419 hints at the simile in the next line.

semina rerum: cf. 9 n. Here the phrase prob. has the Lucretian sense or else means quite vaguely 'seeds of things'.

uiuaci: prob. 'life-giving' here; 'From quickning Earth', Sandys. 420

faciemque . . . : 'and assumed one shape or another in the course 421 of time' (cf. 402 n.).

422   **septemfluus:** because in ancient times the Nile had seven
       mouths; e.g. Sen. *N.Q.* 4, 2, 12: 'sic quoque cum se ripis
       continet Nilus, per septena ostia in mare emittitur'. Nowadays
       the Delta is watered by two branches, the Rosetta and the
       Damietta; the other five survive as canals. The word is
       probably an Ovidian coinage; Catullus and Virgil had used
       septemgeminus, cf. *Aen.* 6, 800, 'septemgemini . . . ostia Nili'.
423   **antiquo:** 'original', see 116 n.

       alueo: the coalescence of the last two vowels is known as
       'synizesis', 'melting together'. Cf. *proinde, prout, eodem, aureo,
       Orphea* etc. See Postgate, *Prosodia Latina* p. 52 f.

       Ovid makes use of a belief about the Nile that was current in
       his own time; see Diodorus 1, 10.
424   **sidere:** = *sole.* The word has the general sense of heavenly
       body and can be applied to sun, moon, planet, fixed star and
       comet. For a good discussion of its usage see R. J. Getty's
       Lucan 1, Appx. A. Cf. *A.A.* 1, 724: 'a radiis sideris esse niger'.

       recens limus: refers to the mud brought down and spread over
       the land by the Nile; Sen. *N.Q.* 4, 2, 9: 'is (Nilus) arenoso et
       sitienti solo et aquam inducit et terram'.
*426   **per ipsum . . . :** goes with *uident.* The peasants see the
       animals during the very time of their coming to birth, i.e.
       when they are making their way from the womb of Mother
       Earth to the air.
428   **numeris:** in the sense of 'members, parts'; Cic. *N.D.* 2, 37:
       'mundus perfectus expletusque omnibus suis numeris atque
       partibus'; *Off.* 3, 14: 'illud officium . . . omnes numeros habet' =
       'perfectum et absolutum est.'
430   **quippe:** 'for in fact'. Ovid only uses this word in the *Met.*
       and the *Tristia.*—**temperiem sumpsere:** = *temperati sunt,* 'have
       been mixed in due proportion'.

       According to Anaximander 'life first arose . . . in the warm
       mud or slime, for the origin of life was in moisture acted upon
       by warmth' (W. K. C. Guthrie, *Greek Philosophers*, London,
       1950, p. 28).
432   **aquae pugnax:** in prose *pugnax* with the dative is Silver
       Latin.

       uapor: not 'steam' but 'heat'. This is always the meaning in
       Lucretius, and often in other authors, e.g. Virg. *Aen.* 5, 682:
       'lentusque carinas est uapor', *Met.* 10, 126: 'solisque uapore'.
433   Anaximander 'saw this present world as a warring concourse

of opposite qualities, of which four were primary—hot and cold, wet and dry' (Guthrie, *op. cit.* p. 26).

discors concordia: Horace has the same oxymoron in *Epist.* 1, 12, 19, and Lucan in 1, 98; cf. Manil. 1, 142: 'discordia concors' and Sen. *N.Q.* 7, 27, 4: 'tota haec mundi concordia ex discordibus constat'.

fetibus aptast: 'favours generation'.

ergo: resumes the story from 421, after the Nile simile and the 434 philosophical interlude; cf. 177 n.

solibus: the plural is often equivalent to 'sunshine', 'sunny 435 days'; cf. Mart. 6, 43, 5: 'Baiani soles', *Met.* 13, 793: 'solibus hibernis . . . gratior'.

alto aestu: a variation of *solibus aetheriis* in chiastic pattern.

recanduit: note the prefix.

species: hence our use of 'species'.   436

antiquas: those that had existed before the Flood.   437

quidem: really emphasises *nollet*, but in such cases is attracted 438 to the pronoun.—**nollet:** sc. *te genuisse.* If she had had a choice in the matter, she would have been unwilling to produce such a monster as the Python.—**te quoque** such apostrophe is often nothing more than a metrical convenience in Latin and here is prob. best translated by the third person.

Python: a dragon supposed to have lived in a cave on Parnassus. The legend here told is prob. aetiological, i.e. it was invented to explain the place-name *Pytho*, the old name of Delphi, and its adj. *Pythian.*

tantum etc.: i.e. 'so large an area of the mountain (Parnassus)'. 440

de: the partitive use frequently found; cf. Cic. *Mil.* 65: 'se gladio percussum esse ab uno de illis', *Tusc.* 4, 16: 'et si quae sunt de genere eodem', Ov. *Fasti* 2, 748: 'quantum de bello dicitur esse super?' It is of course from this that the French *de* derives.

deus arquitenens: Phoebus. The epithet (cf. Gk. τοξοφόρος) *441 was first used by Naevius in his *Bellum Poenicum.*

in dammis: one would expect *in* plus acc. here, but the abl. 442 gives the convenient form *fugacibus*, which by the way is prob. to be taken with both nouns, cf. 66 n.

grauem telis: cf. Plin. *Ep.* 7, 27, 10: 'grauis uinculis', Livy 443 21, 48, 4: 'grauis uolnere'.

Ancient rhetoricians would have regarded this line as an example of ἔμφασις ('in-saying'). Quintilian discusses the figure in 8, 3, 83-86, recognising two types: 'the one means more than it says, the other actually means something that it does not say. Homer provides an example of the first when Menelaus says that the Greeks *descended* into the Wooden Horse; for he indicates its size by a single verb'. So in our passage we infer the dimensions of Apollo from those of his quiver. However by the time we reach the Daphne story the god has shrunk to the size of an ordinary man.

444   **nigra:** black because of the serpent's poison; cf. Virg. *Aen.* 4, 514: 'nigri cum lacte ueneni'; Prop. 2, 27, 10: 'pocula nigra', 'draughts of poison'.

445   **neue:** cf. 72 n.

possit: for this present tense in past sequence cf. Caes. *B.C.* 3, 20, 4: 'legem promulgauit ut creditae pecuniae soluantur', Liv. 3, 28, 1: 'imperauit ut . . . iubeant', and *Met.* 11, 584.

446   **celebri:** suggests both the fame of the games and the crowd that gathered to watch them; in the same way both meanings may be present in Cic. *Div.* 1, 19, 37: 'numquam illud oraculum Delphis tam celebre et tam clarum fuisset . . .'

447   **Pythia:** = τὰ Πύθια; the Pythian games in honour of Apollo were celebrated every four years in mid-August on the Crisaean plain below Delphi and prob. continued, like the Olympic games, until late in the 4th century. The victors were crowned with a garland from the sacred bay-tree in the vale of Tempe. Until 585 B.C., when the games were reorganised by the Amphictionic League (see Bury, *History of Greece*, pp. 157 ff.), the contests were musical, but from then on athletic events also took place.

*de domitae . . . : cf. 14. 433-4: 'Canentem/nomine de nymphae ueteres dixere Camenae'.

448   **iuuenum:** 'athletes'.

manu: covers boxing, wrestling, discus- and spear-throwing.
pedibus: running and jumping.
rota: chariot-racing.

450   **nondum . . . :** because Daphne had not yet been changed into a laurel, or, more correctly, into a bay-tree. The detail about the oak-wreath seems to be an ingenious invention of O.'s to pave the way for the next metamorphosis.

longo . . . crine: Apollo has long hair and no beard to symbolise his eternal youth.

451   **de qualibet:** i.e. 'with leaves from any tree'.

The story of Phoebus and Daphne has touches that remind one 452
of O.'s love poetry and is in lighter and wittier vein than the
previous ones.—The tale of Daphne's transformation was prob.
invented in order to explain why the bay played such an import-
ant part in the cult of Apollo. The bay (in Gk. δάφνη) was
valued for its medicinal properties; the Pythian priestess chewed
its leaves to induce the prophetic trance; it was used in ceremon-
ies of purification; it was the symbol of the poet's calling.—The
story forms the subject of a number of wall-paintings at Pompeii.
In the National Gallery there is a delightful picture by Antonio
Pollaiuolo, the 15th-century Florentine painter, which shows
Daphne at the moment of her transformation.

Peneia: O. makes her daughter of the river Peneus in Thessaly,
which rises in Mt. Pindus and flows into the sea through the vale
of Tempe.

ignara: i.e. *caeca.* 453

Delius: because the island of Delos was Apollo's birthplace. 454

Reminds one of *Am.* 1, 1, 23, where O. says of Cupid: 455
'lunauitque genu sinuosum fortiter arcum'.

cornua: for the explanation of this read Homer's description
of the bow of Pandarus in *Il.* 4, 105 ff. The ancient bow was
made of two horns, often of the ibex, held together by a centre-
piece, usu. a cylindrical metal tube: see the illustration in
Rich.

neruo: the sinew of an ox was often used for this, or horsehair
(cf. *Ex P.* 1, 2, 19).

'quid' que: the *que* is not part of Apollo's words but connects 456
them with what has gone before, cf. 735, 753, 757. This device is
common in O. but rare in other poets.—Here again the form of
the verse is reminiscent of the style of the *Amores:* 'quis tibi,
saeue puer, dedit hoc in carmina iuris?' *Am.* 1, 1, 5.

qui: the antecedent is to be understood from *nostros* 'of us, 458
who . . .'
The line is a good example of the ἀπὸ κοινοῦ construction.
certa uulnera goes with both inf. clauses but has been split up
between the two. 'Vide annon magnifice haec omnia, et ut
decuit mox superbia sua periturum' remarks the Delphin com-
mentator.

tumidum: with poison. Cf. 3, 33 (of another serpent) 'corpus 460
tumet omne uenenis'.

face: Cupid's torch lights the flame of love in the heart. 461

nescioquos: contemptuous, as often; e.g. Cic. *Fin.* 4, 61: 'Platoni ipsi nescioquem illum anteponebas?', 'that nonentity'.

462   **inritare:** cf. 9, 134: 'inritamen amoris'; *Fasti* 2, 649: 'inritat cortice flammas'.

nec: for *neu*, and see 597 n. Common in O.; it also occurs commonly in prose, e.g. Cic. *Off.* 1, 92: 'se utilem praebeat... nec lubidini...pareat'.

adsere: originally a legal term, cf. Liv. 3, 45, 2: 'qui adserantur in libertatem'; *ibid.* 44, 5: 'ut uirginem in seruitutem adsereret'. Then in the general meaning of 'to claim', cf. 761.

464   **te meus arcus:** sc. *figet.*

466   **eliso** etc.: lit. 'forced out by the through-beaten wings'. The phrase gives a good idea of the resistance of the air to the wings as they cut through it. Cf. 8, 339: 'excussis elisi nubibus ignes'; Luc. 7, 475: 'stridulus aer/elisus lituis'.

469   **diuersorum operum:** descriptive genitive—'of contrary effect'.
fugat hoc: sc. *amorem*, of course.

From here until 474 O. develops antithesis: *hoc . . . illud, quod facit . . . quod fugat, hoc . . . illo, alter . . . altera.* Note the parallelism and chiasmus in 470-1 and see it repeated in 481-2.

471   **sub harundine:** 'at the tip of the shaft'. In ancient times arrows were made of the stems of reeds. Pliny (*N.H.* 16, 160), talking of eastern nations where the arrow was the main armament, remarks that almost half the population of the world lives in subjection to the reed. According to him there was no better reed for making arrows than the sort which grew in the Renus at Bononia (Bologna); it had plenty of pith, was of a convenient weight and held to its course in a wind.

473   **medullas:** the marrow represents the inmost soul; cf. *Tr.* 1, 5, 9: 'haec mihi semper erunt imis infixa medullis', Eur. *Hipp.* 255, πρὸς ἄκρον μυελὸν ψυχῆς.

Apo! ineas: cf. 413 n.

474   **nomen amantis:** O. prob. does not mean that she shrank from being called a lover, but that she shrank from lovers in general, from the idea of a lover. Cic. *Off.* 3, 101: 'utilitatis nomen non tam splendidum quam necessarium ducimus', 'the idea of expediency'; *ibid.* 70: 'fidei bonae nomen existimabat manare latissime', 'he thought that the idea of good faith had far-reaching consequences'.

475   For the piling up of genitives cf. 13, 550: 'non oblita animorum, annorum oblita suorum'.

uitta: a ribbon, or fillet, was worn by all free-born girls and 477
married women. The unmarried wore it differently from the
married, but the details are uncertain.

positos sine lege:=*inornatos* (497); Daphne had no fancy
hair-style. For this meaning of *sine lege* cf. *A.A.* 3, 133, ff.:
'munditiis capimur. non sint sine lege capilli: / admotae
formam dantque negantque manus. / nec genus ornatus
unumst' etc. So *ornare* is used absolutely in *Am.* 2, 7, 17:
'sollers ornare Cypassis', referring to her ability in doing hair;
A.A. 3, 239: 'tuta sit ornatrix', i.e. the maid who specialises in
coiffure.

The line contains more elisions than O. usu. allows himself. 478
Cf. Cat. 62, 42: 'multi illum pueri, multae optauere puellae . . .'
and O.'s reminiscence of that in 3, 353 ff. 'multi illum iuuenes,
multae cupiere puellae . . .'

uiri: goes with *impatiens* as well as *expers*; cf. *Fasti* 6, 288: 479
'impatiens restitit una uiri'.

auia: just like our 'out-of-the-way.'

lustrat: in this sense of 'frequent, wander through' occurs in
prose also, e.g. Cic. *Fin.* 5, 87: 'cur ipse Pythagoras Aegyptum
lustrauit?'

Hymen: first means the marriage song sung by the procession 480
escorting the bride to her new home, then the god of marriage.
The first syllable can be long: *Her.* 12, 137: 'ut subito nostras
Hymen cantatus ad aures / uenit'.   481

     Cf. 325-6 n.   -2

taedas: torches made of pitch-pine. In ancient weddings the 483
bride was escorted to the bridegroom's house in the evening by
the light of torches, cf. Homer's picture of a wedding on the
shield of Achilles, *Il.* 18, 491-6.

Cf. Virg. *Georg.* 1, 430: 'at si uirgineum suffuderit ore 484
ruborem'. For the pluperfect cf. 610 *praesenserat.*

inque patris . . . ceruice: when a noun with a prep. has a gen. 485
dependent on it the prep. is often placed with the gen., e.g. 8,
805-6: 'pendere putares/pectus et a spinae tantummodo crate
teneri'. In the same way you find such arrangements as: *Fasti*
5, 551: 'ultor ad ipse suos caelo descendit honores'; *Tr.* 4, 8,
11-12: 'inque / securus patria consenuisse mea'. These are exten-
sions of the common prose bracketing order; e.g. Cic. *Clu.* 46:
'ad eorum se familiaritatem . . . applicarat'. Cf. 35 n. and 706.

ceruice: always in the plural in the prose of Cicero and Sallust (cf. 542). Livy and Silver Age prose writers use both sing. and pl.

486-7 A reminiscence of Callimachus, who, in line 6 of his Hymn to Artemis makes her say to Zeus: δός μοι παρθενίην αἰώνιον, ἄππα, φυλάσσειν. O. must have known Callimachus' poetry well. If more of it had survived, we should no doubt have been able to recognise many more reminiscences of this sort. If we tend to emphasise originality in poetry, the ancients delighted in recognition, in being able to say: 'This is that, though with a difference'.

488   quidem . . . sed: the equivalent in Latin of the Gk. μέν . . . δέ; cf. 209-10; 438 etc. But Latin most commonly uses asyndeton to express such contrast; see Hardie, *Latin Prose*, p. 30, sec. 35.
        te: cf. 438 n.

489   uotoque . . . : note how this is simply a variation of the previous phrase. In poetry designed primarily to be heard you have to make sure that your points are fully understood by the audience. See also 628 n.

491   The god of prophecy cannot foresee his own future; cf. 523-4.

492   Cf. Virg. *Georg.* 1, 85: 'leuem stipulam crepitantibus urere flammis'; Page in his note on 86 explains why burning the stubble increases the fertility of the soil.
        aristis: the ancient reaper cut fairly close to the ear, leaving perhaps two-thirds of the stalk behind.
        adolentur: more often used in a religious connexion; e.g. Lucr. 4, 1237: 'adolentque altaria donis'; *Aen.* 3, 547: 'Iunoni Argiuae iussos adolemus honores'.

493   Cf. *Fasti* 4, 167: 'semiustamque facem uigilata nocte uiator / ponet'. Duff on Juv. 3, 285 notes that there was no system of street-lighting even in Rome.

494   admouit: sc. *saepibus*.
        sub luce: *sub* with the abl. or acc. gives a rough approximation of time when; cf. Caes. *B.G.* 7, 61: 'sub lucem'.

495   abiit: cf. 236 n.

496   sterilem: because, of course, Daphne did not reciprocate.

497   inornatos: cf. 477 n. 'Hir haire unkembd about hir necke downe flaring he did see', Golding.

498   comantur: cf. *Her.* 21, 88: 'comuntur nostrae matre iubente comae', Mart. 12, 82, 9: 'exiguos secto comentem dente capillos'. The word is commoner in the perf. part. pass. *comptus*; e.g. *Am.* 1, 1, 20: 'longas compta puella comas'.

oscula: 'little mouth'. A charming word; O. uses it pathetically 499
in 13, 491: 'lacrimas in uolnera fundit / osculaque ore tegit
consuetaque pectora plangit'. It occurs in Silver Latin prose,
see the Pliny quotation in 320 n. and Petr. *Sat.* 126, fin.:
'osculum quale Praxiteles habere Dianam credidit'.—'He view'd
her Lips, too sweet to view alone', Dryden.

bracchia: the fore-arm; *lacertos:* the upper arm. 501

plus: adverbial acc. The full phrase would be *nudos plus
quam media parte*, 'bare more than by half'. *quam* is often
omitted after *plus, amplius* and *minus*.

siqua latent . . .: 'Believes the Beauties yet unseen are best', 502
Dryden. A remark that might be applied to critics and com-
mentators too.

ad: 'at', cf. 3, 245: 'ad nomen caput ille refert', Livy 9, 7, 7: 503
'ad famam obsidionis dilectus haberi coeptus erat', id. 42, 67,
12: 'ad horum preces in Boeotiam duxit'.

An amusing declaration of love, delivered on the run. Cupid 504
certainly succeeds in making the great Python-killer look rather
foolish. 'Non bene conueniunt nec in una sede morantur /
maiestas et amor' remarks Lemaire, quoting 2, 846.—Apollo's
speech is very reminiscent of O.'s elegiac love poetry. It is
interesting to watch how O. works out three simple ideas:
'Stop! I love you! I am Apollo'. 504-11 elaborate the first two,
512-24 the third. We can trace one method of this elaboration in
504-7 and 512-5. 'non insequor hostis' (504) is followed by three
illustrations ('sic agna lupum' etc.) and reappears in positive
guise as 'amor est . . . sequendi' (507). Similarly 'cui placeas
inquire' (512) reappears negatively as 'nescis temeraria' etc...
(514) with three denials sandwiched in between.

The weak caesura in the third foot is noteworthy. There are
six examples of it in the eighteen lines from 504 to 521: the others
are 505, 508, 512, 515, 521. Clearly it is used to express the hurry
of the race (cf. 541).

'With flittring fethers sillie doues so from the Goshauke flie', 506
Golding.

prona: cf. 84 n. 508

moderatius insequar ipse: few but O. would have thought of 511
this incongruous idea.

cui placeas: *placeo* is frequent in Roman love poetry in this 512
sense. Cf. the phrase 'tu mihi sola places' in Tib. 4, **13**, 3,
Prop. 2, 7, 19, and *A.A.* 1, 42.

514 **horridus:** like *rusticus* 'uncouth, gauche', though stronger: 'No homebred Clowne', Sandys. Contrast the use in *Am.* 2, 16, 19: 'si premerem uentosas horridus Alpes', 'shivering with cold'.

   obseruo: cf. Pl. *Mil.* 328: 'at ego ilico obseruo fores'. Compound for the more usual simple verb; Virg. *Aen.* 6, 338: 'dum sidera seruat'.

516 **Claros:** on the Ionian coast near Colophon, with a temple and oracle of Apollo. Germanicus consulted this oracle in A.D. 18 and it was rumoured that the priest foretold his early death (see Tac. *Ann.* 2, 54).

   Tenedos: the island off the coast of the Troad, with a temple dedicated to Sminthian Apollo.

   Patara: on the coast of Lycia, due east of Rhodes; St. Paul touched there on his return journey from Macedonia (see *Acts* XXI, 1).

518 **concordant:** a rare word and in classical Latin always intransitive; therefore the subject here will be *carmina*—'songs harmonise with the strings (of the lyre)'. *neruis* is prob. dative; the more usu. construction is *cum*,e. g. Sen. *Ep.* 75, 4: 'concordet sermo cum uita'.

519 **certa:** cf. 458.

   sagitta: might be nom. or abl., but is prob. the former.

520 **uacuo:** 'empty' in the sense that it is free from love; cf. Prop. 1, 10, 30; 'qui numquam uacuo pectore liber erit'.

521 **inuentum:** cf. 210 n. *admissum.*

   opifer: first occurs in Ennius.

523 Cf. Prop. 2, 1, 57-8: 'omnes humanos sanat medicina dolores; / solus amor morbi non habet artificem', and *Her.* 5, 149: 'me miseram quod amor non est medicabilis herbis'.

524 **domino:** 'possessor'.—Ovid's version of *Physician, heal thyself*. He seizes on such contradictions with delight, cf. 491: 'suaque illum oracula fallunt'.—'And his own Physick the Physician fails', Dryden.

526 At first sight this seems to contradict 503, but in fact *fugit=* 'outdistanced'. Daphne had increased her speed, as Phoebus proceeds to do in 532, *admisso . . . passu.*

   cumque ipso: i.e. 'left him and his unfinished words'. For this use of *cum* cf. 56, 217. Contrast Livy 6, 10, 5: 'oppidum cum praesidio relictum'.

527 **tum quoque uisa decens** appears again in heightened form as 'auctaque forma fugast' in 530, and three descriptive clauses are

sandwiched between; cf. 504 n. Note the parallel endings of 527 and 528 (cf. 372 n.). Ovid rings the changes on *uenti, flamina* and *aura*.

Cf. 2, 875: 'tremulae sinuantur flamine uestes'.   528

sed enim: 'however', cf. Virg. *Aen.* 1, 19: 'progeniem sed enim 530 Troiano a sanguine duci / audierat'. *enim* has here its original intensive force, 'indeed, in fact, truly'. Compare the use of *uerum enim*, Ter. *Phorm.* 555: 'saluos est ut opinor; uerum enim metuo malum'.

non sustinet ultra: 'cannot longer endure'; cf. 6, 367: 'nec dicere sustinet ultra / uerba minora dea'.

monebat: Cupid is at Phoebus' elbow, egging him on.   531

admisso: 'headlong'. Cf. Caes. *B.C.* 2, 34: 'admissis equis', 532 'giving free rein to their horses, at a gallop'; *Her.* 2, 114: 'et sacer admissas exigit Hebrus aquas'. 'his racing stream'.

This extremely vivid simile should be compared with Virgil's 533ff in *Aen.* 12, 749 ff. O.'s gains in piquancy if we remember Daphne's predilection for hunting; she is now the hunted. Golding's translation is delightful:

'And euen as when the greedie greihund doth course the sillie Hare

Amids the plaine and champion field without all couert bare,

Both twaine of them do straine themselues and lay on footemanship,

Who may best runne with all his force the toother to outstrip,

The tone for safetie of his life, the toother for his pray,

The greihund ay prest with open mouth to beare the Hare away,

Thrusts foorth his snout, and girdeth out, and at hir loines dooth snatch,

As though he would at euerie stride betweene his teeth hir latch:

Againe in doubt of being caught the Hare ay shrinking slips,

Upon the sudden from his iawes, and from betweene his lips.'

canis Gallicus: prob. the greyhound, which hunts by sight (hence *uacuo*, 'open').

hic here refers to the further noun, *ille* to the nearer; cf. 534 539, 697.

inhaesuro: i.e. about to dig in his teeth.   535

iam iamque: 'every moment'. O. more commonly uses the form *iam iam*; cf. *Her.* 10, 83: 'iam iam uenturos aut hac aut suspicor illac', *Tr.* 1, 2, 20: 'iam iam tacturos sidera summa putes'.

536 **uestigia**: not the hare's footprints, but=*pedes*. Cf. Plin. *N.H.* 10, 202: 'feles quam leuibus uestigiis obrepunt auibus'; 4, 343: 'summa pedum taloque tenus uestigia tingit'.

extento rostro: 'with his straining muzzle'.

537 **in ambiguost**: more usu. impersonal, e.g. Pl. *Trin.* 594: 'in ambiguost etiam nunc quid ea re fuat' ('what has happened to it'); cf. 396 'in dubiost'.

an: regularly used in Classical Latin after certain words to introduce an indirect question, e.g. *scio, nescio, dubito, tempto, quaero.* In later Latin *an* ousted *num* almost entirely.

538 **eripitur**: middle use—'tears herself away'.

541 The weak caesura combined with the short sentences backs up the meaning, giving the effect of speed; cf. 286, 504 n.

542 **imminet**: cf. 146 n.

adflat: Homer has a similar picture when describing the foot-race between Ajax and Odysseus (*Il.* 23, 765-6): κὰδ δ' ἄρα οἱ κεφαλῆς χέ' ἀυτμένα δῖος 'Οδυσσεὺς / αἰεὶ ῥίμφα θέων.

543 **expalluit illa**: 'The colour faded in hir cheekes'. Golding. The caesural pause in the fifth foot suggests the sudden failure of Daphne's strength. For a similar effect see Virg. *Georg.* 4, 491: 'immemor heu uictusque animi respexit. ibi omnis . . .'

*544 **uicta labore fugae**: cf. 5, 618: 'fessa labore fugae'.

549 **praecordia**:=*pectora*.

libro: usu. thin rind, whereas *cortex* is generally the rough outer bark.

551 **uelox pigris**: such placing together of contrasted words is a favourite device in Latin; e.g. 51: 'frigore flamma' 208 'sermone silentia', 355 'duo turba', 432 'ignis aquae', 433 'discors concordia', etc.—The spondees and the consonants *x p* and *s r* coming together in this line slow down the pronunciation and help to make more vivid the idea of Daphne's feet sticking fast. Sandys achieves a similar effect by using monosyllables: 'And late swift feet, now rootes, are less than slow'.

552 **ora cacumen habet**: cf. 6, 144: 'cetera uenter habet'.

nitor: Dryden translates 'The smoothness of her Skin remains alone'; cf. Hor. *Carm.* 1, 19, 5: 'urit me Glycerae nitor / splendentis Pario marmore purius'. The word aptly describes the glossiness of the bay-leaf; cf. 14, 720. 'nitidaque incingere lauru'.

unus:=*solus*, cf. 583 and Caes. *B.G.* 4, 16: 'Ubii qui uni legatos miserant'.

hanc: prob. refers to *arborem*, or *laurum* implied in the pre- 553
vious lines.

A typically Ovidian idea, like 556. Notice the rhythm of the 554
line.

ut membra: cf. 567 'utque caput'. 555

nostrae: to be taken with *coma* and *citharae* as well. 559

ducibus Latiis: the Roman general celebrating a triumph wore 560
a garland of bay and carried a bay branch. The bay was the sign
of victory. *Litterae laureatae* announced successes in the field to
the Senate.—O. is fond of bringing in Roman references; cf.
145, 173 ff, 201 ff.

Triumphum: cf. *Am.* 1, 2, 25: 'populo clamante Triumphum'.
The people would shout 'Io Triumphe'; *ibid.* 34: 'uolgus "io"
magna uoce "Triumphe" canet'. For the accusative representing
a vocative cf. 12, 215: 'ecce canunt Hymenaeon'=*A.A.* 1, 563:
' "Hymenaee" canunt'.

longas: first came senators and magistrates followed by 561
trumpeters, then the spoils and emblems of the conquered
peoples, representations of their towns, fortresses, rivers etc.,
then victims for the sacrifice, then the crowd of prisoners, the
general's lictors in their purple tunics, musicians, and finally the
general himself in the triumphal chariot at the head of his troops.

Capitolia: for the plural cf. *Palatia* 176.—The procession
started from the Campus Martius and proceeded by way of the
Porta Triumphalis, Circus Flaminius, Velabrum, Forum
Boarium, Circus Maximus, and Via Sacra, to the Capitol.

postibus: place where. For *Augustis* used adjectivally cf. 15, 562
869: 'caput Augustum'.

eadem: equivalent to 'also'; cf. *Tr.* 2, 266: 'nil prodest quod
non laedere possit idem'.

Two laurels grew outside the entrance to Augustus' palace on 563
the Palatine. A wreath of oak-leaves hung over the door.
This was the 'civic crown' awarded for saving the life of a
comrade in battle and voted to Augustus as the saviour of his
people; cf. *Fasti* 1, 614; 4, 953-4; *Tr.* 3, 1, 35 ff. and Owen's note.

The line-ending echoes 449; cf. 87 n. 565

Paean: there is point in calling Apollo the Healer here. He 566
has given the story a happy ending after all. Cf. 390: 'Pro-
methides . . . Epimethida'.

factis modo: cf. *Tr.* 3, 7, 25: 'aut ego praebebam factis modo
uersibus aures'.

568- An ingenious bridge-passage linking the story of Daphne
585 with that of Io. O. imagines the rivers visiting Peneus after
Daphne's transformation, uncertain whether to offer him sym-
pathy or congratulations. But Inachus, the Argive river, was
not among these visitors; he was in mourning for the loss of his
daughter Io.

568 **nemus:** almost=*saltus* here, 'glen'. The two words are
often coupled together; cf. Virg. *Ecl.* 6, 56: 'nemorum saltus',
Ov. *A.A.* 1, 311: 'in nemus et saltus', *Fasti* 4, 104: 'quem toti
saltus, quem nemus omne tremit'.—Livy (44, 6) calls Tempe a
saltus.

Haemoniae:=Thessaly.

praerupta silua: in translating we should prob. turn noun into
adj. and vice versa. Cf. Cat. 64, 286: 'Tempe, quae siluae
cingunt super impendentes'.

*569 **Tempe:** 'In truth the natural features of the pass of Tempe are
well fitted to impress the mind with a religious awe . . . The
traveller who descends into the deep gorge . . . is confronted on
either hand only by a stupendous wall of mighty precipices
shooting up in prodigious grandeur and approaching each other
in some places so near that they almost seem to meet . . . The
cliffs on the side of Olympus . . . in rainy weather . . . are
rendered still more impressive by the waterfalls that pour down
their sides to swell the smooth and steady current of the stream'
(Frazer, *Folklore in the O.T.* vol. 1, p. 172).

For ancient descriptions of this famous ravine see Livy 44, 6,
and Pl. *N.H.* 4, 31. Pliny's picture of the river is worth tran-
scribing: 'hac labitur Penius, uiridis calculo, amoenus circa
ripas gramine, canorus auium concentu'.—O. has a keen eye for
natural beauty and his short descriptions of scenery are often
very well done: e.g. *A.A.* 3, 687-94; *Met.* 3, 155 ff., 407 ff.;
5, 385 ff.; 11, 229 ff.

571 **deiectuque graui:** 'by the weight of its fall'.

tenues . . . nubila: 'shifting clouds of smoke-like mist'.

572 **summisque adspergine siluis:** effective alliteration. *siluis* is of
course dative.

573 **plus quam uicina:** i.e. *etiam longinqua.*

fatigat: so Philoctetes 'wearies' the rocks of Lemnos with his
cries: 'uoce fatigaret Lemnia saxa sua' *Tr.* 5, 1, 62.—'Amidst thy
desert walks the lapwing flies, / And *tires* their echoes with
unvaried cries', Goldsmith, *Deserted Village*, 45-6.

haec domus . . .: this is the type of Latin expression that lies 574
behind Milton's 'Is this the region, this the soil, the clime . . .'
  in his: sc. *penetralibus*, i.e. in the vale of Tempe—'here'.   575
  antro: place where, with *residens*.
  iura dabat: Nettleship (*Contrib.* under *Ius*) says that the 576
phrase means 'give decisions', and so is almost equivalent to
'govern'; cf. Virg. *Aen.* 1, 293: 'cana Fides et Vesta Remo cum
fratre Quirinus iura dabunt'. The converse, *iura petere*, is thus
equivalent to 'be under the jurisdiction of'; cf. Livy 23, 5, 13:
'ex Africa et a Carthagine iura petere'.
  popularia: for the meaning 'local, native', cf. Hor. *Carm.* 2, 577
13, 24-5: 'Aeoliis fidibus querentem / Sappho puellis de
popularibus', Ov. *Met.* 11, 54: 'flumen populare relinquunt'.
The word can be used as a noun to mean 'fellow-citizen', e.g.
Cic. *Ac.* 2, 118: 'hoc Anaximandro, populari et sodali suo, non
persuasit'. But *populares* most often means 'democrats' as
opposed to *optimates*.
  nescia gratentur: cf. 222: 'experiar deus hic . . . an sit mortalis'. 578
In prose too the particle can be omitted from the first member of
a disjunctive question; e.g. Cic. *Fin.* 4, 69: 'si nihil interesse
nostra putemus ualeamus aegrine simus'; Livy 5, 28, 5: 'adeo ut
in incerto fuerit . . . uicissent uictine essent'.
  Sperchios: flows into the Malian Gulf. *Enipeus* and *Apidanos**579
are tributaries of the Peneus. *Amphrysos* flows into the Pegas- -80
aean Gulf. *Aias* an Illyrian river that rises on Mt. Lacmon.
  populifer and **irrequietus** are adjectives that first appear in O.
  senex: cf. 'Old Father Thames', and 645 *senior Inachus.*
  alii) (*popularia.*   581
  qua: abl. of road by which, cf. 170 *hac.*
  impetus: equivalent to 'current', cf. Livy 21, 28, 2: 'nite-
bantur perrumpere impetum fluminis'.
  Inachus: first king of Argos; he gave his name to the Argive 583
river Inachus.
  unus: see 552 n.
  fletibus auget aquas: for this conceit cf. 11, 47-8 on the death 584
of Orpheus: 'lacrimis quoque flumina dicunt / increuisse
suis'.
  Io: a popular theme with the ancient poets. Aeschylus
introduces her into the *P.V.* Sophocles composed a tragedy
called *Inachus.* Horace mentions her in *A.P.* 124 in company
with other common heroes and heroines of the drama. O.

himself had told the story before in *Her.* 14, 85-108, and our passage has several reminiscences of the earlier version. Later, Valerius Flaccus re-worked the theme in *Argonautica* 4, 351-418, taking many hints from Ovid.—The story has been variously interpreted. Herodotus gives a rationalistic explanation at the beginning of his History; he says that according to the Persians Io was kidnapped by Phoenician traders who were on a visit to Argos and was carried off to Egypt. Others see in Io a personification of the moon; the crescent moon is symbolised by the heifer's horns; her wanderings figure the moon's course through the sky; Argus, with his many eyes, represents the starry heavens. Others again regard Io as a secondary form of Hera, whose epithet in Homer is βοῶπις, 'ox-eyed', supporting this view by the fact that in some forms of the legend Io is said to be Hera's priestess. Argus on this interpretation would be a subordinate male divinity, and Hermes would have been introduced to explain the epithet ἀργειφόντης (usually translated 'Argus-slayer') so often applied to him.

Fortunately our enjoyment of Ovid's story does not depend on any of these interpretations. Like the Daphne episode it is an exquisite mixture of humour and pathos. We have evidence of Ovid's love of the bizarre (e.g. 626-7, 649, 739 ff.), of his humour (601 ff.) and of his vivid and sympathetic imagination (630 ff., 730-1, 746). Wit and pathos are combined in the epitaph that he makes for Argus (720-1).

586 **apud Manes:** 'among the shades'. *manes* can mean (i) the gods of the underworld (ii) the spirits of the dead (cf. 7, 206: 'manesque exire sepulcris'), (iii) an individual ghost, e.g. Livy 3, 58, 11: 'manes Verginiae'.

587 **esse . . . nu quam:** there is a slight play, for the phrase is idiomatic in the sense of 'to be no more, to be dead'; cf. Hor. *Sat.* 2, 5, 101-2: 'ergo nunc Dama sodalis / nusquam est?'

peiora: the worse of the two alternatives. The whole phrase is a variation of *esse putat nusquam.*—For the elision at the caesura cf. 166 n.

588 **redeuntem:** cf. 698.

590-1 A favourite Ovidian turn; cf. *A.A.* 2, 131: 'ille leui uirga (uirgam nam forte tenebat)', *ib'd.* 135: 'campus erat (campumque facit), *A.A.* 3, 53-4: 'dixit et e myrto (myrto nam uincta capillos / constiterat) folium granaque pauca dedit'. It gives an impression of spontaneity and ease, of the speaking voice. Cf. 597.

medio orbe: 'in mid-course'; cf. Cic. *Tim.* 32: 'ubi sol suum 592 totum confecit et peragrauit orbem'.

nemorum secreta: this use of the neuter adj. as a noun with the 594 partitive genitive is common in the poets, Livy and post-Augustan prose; e.g. Virg. *Aen.* 5, 695: 'ardua terrarum', Livy 30, 2: 'incerta belli', Tac. *Ann.* 1, 61: 'occulta saltuum'.

de plebe: cf. Livy 5, 39: 'de plebe multitudo', Cic. *Arch.* 25: 595 'malus poeta de populo', *Fasti* 5, 20: 'de media plebe . . . deus', and 173 n.

magna: abl., of course.

uaga: because they range through space. Cf. πλάνητες 596 ἀστέρες ('wandering stars'), hence our word 'planets', as opposed to fixed stars. So Horace has *uaga luna* (*Sat.* 1, 8, 21).

ne fuge: *ne* with the second person of the imperative occurs 597 in Plautus and Terence, and would therefore seem to be colloquial usage in their time. The Augustan poets adopted it, but it was avoided by the prose-writers. There is however a solitary example of it in Livy 3, 2, 9: 'erit copia pugnandi, ne timete'.

Lernae: a marshy district south of Argos.

Lyrcea: Lyrceus was a mountain on the western boundary of 598 Argolis. There was a town called Lyrcea on the N. bank of the Inachus not far from Mycenae. Of course from O.'s point of view the exact location of these places does not matter; cf. 217 n.

consita: cf. Livy 33, 6, 7: 'ager consitus crebris arboribus'.

inducta: this participle normally agrees with the thing that is 599 spread over, cf. *A.A.* 3, 199: 'inducta candorem quaerere creta', *Met.* 11, 231: 'summis inductum est aequor harenis'.

Juno can generally be relied on to cause trouble, and O. here *601 makes her appearance the pretext for a humorous interlude.

uolucres: for this use of the adj. Ehwald compares Virg. *Georg.* 602 2, 217: 'fumosque uolucres'.

die: *dies* is often equivalent to 'sun' or 'sky', e.g. Lucr. 1, 147: 603 'lucida tela diei', *Her.* 19, 122: 'latet obscura condita nube dies', Livy 22, 6, 9: 'cum dispulsa nebula aperuisset diem'.

fluminis:=*flumineas*, a slight extension of the possessive genitive; cf. Cic. *Fam.* 9, 16, 4: 'hic uersus Plauti non est'.

ut quae: like *quippe quae, utpote quae.* 605

nosset:=*nouisset*. The technical term for such contraction is 606 *syncope.* It represents the pronunciation of the word in ordinary conversation. It is particularly common with perfect forms; e.g. 152: *adfectasse,* 158: *animasse.* For other examples cf.

dextra, uinclum, oraclum, repostus. Naturally such variant forms were useful to poets.

furta: common in the sense of 'amorous intrigues'; cf. 2, 423: 'hoc certe furtum coniunx mea nesciet'.

607 **aut ego fallor . . . :** 'either I am wrong or I am being wronged'.

610-11 Rhythmically parallel lines with the ghost of a rhyme at the end.—The subject of *praesenserat* is of course *ille* from the next line.

Inachidos: Greek genitive; cf. 218: *Arcados,* 668 *Phoronidos.*

612 **bos quoque formosast:** like 527: 'tum quoque uisa decens'. A favourite idea of Ovid's. Ehwald quotes *Am.* 2, 5, 43: 'spectabat terram: terram spectare decebat', *A.A.* 1, 533: 'clamabat flebatque simul, sed utrumque decebat', *Met.* 4, 230: 'ipse timor decuit', 7, 730, *Fasti* 5, 608. Add *Fasti* 2, 757: 'hoc ipsum decuit; lacrimae decuere pudicam'.

Saturnia: Juno was daughter of Saturn.

613 **quamquam inuita:** *quamquam* with adjectives and participles is common in Silver Latin; in Cicero extremely rare. Cf. 629: 'quamuis auersus'.

nec non, *nec non et,* strengthened forms of 'and', are common in poetry; e.g. Virg. *Georg.* 2, 53: 'nec non et sterilis . . .', *Met.* 7, 230: 'nec non Peneos nec non Spercheides undae', 15, 427: 'nec non et Cecropis nec non Amphionis arces'.

615 **e terra:** cf. 416-7. *terrae filius* was a proverbial expression for a man whose origin was unknown; cf. Tertullian *Apol.* 10: 'nam et terrae filios uulgus uocat quorum genus incertum est' (with Mayor's note).

auctor: is the person responsible for anything. Jupiter was anxious that Juno's enquiries into the heifer's origin should cease.

617 **addicere:** 'surrender, abandon'. A legal term in origin; 'to adjudge, make over', cf. Pl. *Poen.* 185: 'ubi in ius uenerit, addicet praetor familiam totam tibi'; also used of auctioning, 'to knock down', cf. Cic. *Verr.* 2, 1, 144: 'addicitur id opus HS DLX milibus'. Only here in O.

618 **suspectumst:** we should say '*would* arouse suspicion', cf. 214 n. For *suspectum* cf. Caes. *B.G.* 5, 54, 4: 'nulla fere ciuitas fuerit non suspecta nobis'.

pudor . . . amor: such mental conflict is a favourite theme with O. He develops it at large in the following soliloquies: 7, 11 ff.

Medea; 8, 44 ff. Scylla, 481 ff. Althaea; 9, 474 ff. Byblis. Heinze believes that these Ovidian monologues derive ultimately from Greek tragedy, in particular from Euripides *Medea* 364-409 and 1019 80 (*Ovids elegische Erzählung* p. 121).

sociae generis . . .: cf. Virg. *Aen.* 1, 46-7: 'Iouisque / et soror et 620 coniunx'.

poterat: the indicative of verbs expressing duty, propriety or 621 possibility is regularly used in the apodosis of unfulfilled conditions, e.g. Livy 32, 12: 'deleri totus exercitus potuit, si fugientes persecuti uictores essent'; Juv. 10, 123-4: 'Antoni gladios potuit contemnere, si sic / omnia dixisset'. See Madvig 348 (e).

non: goes closely with *uacca*. The combination of the negative with a noun is rare, but cf. *Met.* 5, 61: 'et comes et ueri non dissimulator amoris'.

exuit: cf. *Am.* 3, 4, 43-4: 'uultusque seueros / exue', Cic. 622 *Att.* 13, 2, 1: 'humanitatem omnem exuimus'.

-que: 'but'; cf. 15 n. 623

furti: cf. 606 n.

Arestoridae: the only occurrence of this patronymic in Latin 624 poetry. Arestor was a shadowy Argive hero.

centum . . . cinctum: for the similarity of sound cf. 489: 625 'uetat uotoque', 633: 'toro terrae', 739: 'fitque quod ante fuit'.

inde: 'of these'; cf. Plaut. *Mil.* 711: 'dant inde partem mihi', 626 *Met.* 13, 829: 'lac mihi semper adest niueum: pars inde bibenda / seruatur . . .' The French *en* derives from this word.

suis uicibus: 'in their turn', cf. 4, 218: 'noxque uicem peragit', 'night takes her turn, completes her round'.

seruabant: the word is used absolutely as in 684, cf. Pl. *Most.* 627 451: 'nemo in aedibus seruat'; it is prob. from the military vocabulary. *serua* is frequent in the comedians in the sense of 'look out, take care', cf. Gk. φυλάττου.

in statione: 'on duty, at their post'; another military phrase. Cf. Caes. *B.C.* 1, 43: 'quae in statione pro castris erant Afranii cohortes'; Cic. *Sen.* 73: 'de praesidio et statione uitae decedere'.

Ovidian repetition to drive the point home. 628-9

luce: 'by daylight', cf. Cic. *Rosc. Am.* 56: 'quodsi luce quoque 630 canes latrent'; *Off.* 3, 93: 'ut luce palam in foro saltet'.

indigno: because she did not deserve such treatment. A 631 common use of the adjective in poetry. We might translate 'innocent'. Cf. *Am.* 3, 9, 3: 'flebilis indignos, Elegia, solue capillos', *Tr.* 1, 3, 18: 'imbre per indignas usque cadente genas'.

uincula: not necessarily a chain (*catena*), but anything that binds or fastens; Nep. *Paus.* 4, 1: 'uincla epistulae laxauit', *Fasti* 2, 321: 'tunicarum uincla relaxat', *Met.* 8, 226: 'odoratas, pennarum uincula, ceras'.

632 A reminiscence of a line from the *Io* of Licinius Calvus: 'a, uirgo infelix, herbis pasceris amaris'. Cf. *Her.* 14, 96: 'fronde leuas nimiam caespitibusque famem'; *Daniel* iv, 33: 'The same hour was the thing fulfilled upon Nebuchadnezzar: and he was driven from men, and did eat grass as oxen, and his body was wet with the dew of heaven, till his hairs were grown like eagles' feathers, and his nails like birds' claws'.

633 **proque toro:** 'And in the sted of costlie couch and good soft fetherbed' is Golding's expansion.

635-6 For the repetition cf. 325 n. Here the effect is one of pathos, as in 639-40: 'ripas . . . Inachidas ripas', and 642-3. For the thought cf. 3, 723: 'non habet infelix quae matri bracchia tendat'.

*637 See Critical Notes.

640 **Inachidas:** note that the final *a* is short by nature, cf. 369, 544. For this Gk. form of feminine adjective cf. *Her.* 2, 6: 'Sithonis unda', *ib.* 3, 126: 'Pelias hasta'.

641 Cf. 638.

exsternata: a rare and purely poetical word. The usual compound is *consternare*, which is often used of animals; cf. Livy 37, 41, 10: 'haec uelut procella . . . ita consternauit equos ut repente uelut effrenati passim incerto cursu ferrentur'; Suet. *Ner.* 48: 'equo ex odore cadaueris consternato'.

se refugit: contrast the clever description of Ixion in 4, 461: 'uoluitur Ixion et se sequiturque fugitque'.

642-3 The facility with which O. constructs these word patterns is remarkable. It is not mere virtuosity, however. Here the repetition expresses the pathetic persistence of Io's attempts to make herself known.

644 **patitur tangi:** understand *se* from the following clause.

seque admirantibus offert: i.e. much to their surprise she thrusts herself upon them. For the expression cf. Virg. *Aen*.6, 291: 'strictamque aciem uenientibus offert'; Cic. *Div.* 1, 79: 'ipsi (sc. di) se nobis non offerunt'.

645 **senior:** cf. *senex* 580. The comparative is used for the positive, cf. *Tr.* 4, 8, 3: 'iam subeunt anni fragiles et inertior aetas', Mart. 5, 6, 3· 'serior et beata . . . senectus', and the use of

ocius, saepius. In Late Latin the word was used as a respectful form of address, hence Fr. *seigneur*, It. *signor*, Sp. *señor* etc.

patriis: cf. 413 n.   646

nec retinet lacrimas: 'And in the language of her eyes, she 647 spoke', Dryden.

sequantur: cf. 11, 326: 'lingua tacet, nec uox temptataque uerba sequuntur'; Virg. *Aen.* 12, 912: 'nec uox aut uerba sequuntur'.

oret: for this vivid use of the present subjunctive to represent 648 an unfulfilled condition in the past cf. Virg. *Aen.* 5, 325: 'spatia et si plura supersint,/transeat elapsus prior' (Madvig 347, Obs. 3).

littera pro uerbis: shows that *uerbum* in Latin means primarily 649 the *spoken* word. *littera* is, of course, singular for plural.

duxit: 'traced', cf. *Tr.* 2, 454: 'et tacitam mensae duxit in orbe notam', *Ex P.* 4, 2, 24: 'ducitur et digitis littera rara meis'.

indicium . . . peregit: cf. *Am.* 3, 14, 12: 'commissi perages 650 indiciumque tui'—'provide evidence'.

triste: it is just possible that there may be a double meaning here. The word IO is in Greek often a cry of grief (ἰώ), and sometimes in Latin, e.g. *Fasti* 4, 447: 'io, carissima mater,/auferor'.

inque gementis . . . ingeminat: cf. 625 n.—For *pendens in* cf 651 *Ex P.* 1, 6, 38: 'atque aliquis pendens in cruce uota facit', Virg. *Ecl.* 1, 37: 'cui pendere sua patereris in arbore poma'.

The order is 'tune es (ea) nata quam quaesiui'; *nata* is nomina- 653 tive, not vocative.

reperta: is of course abl. of comparison after *leuior*. There are 654 two possible interpretations of the sentence, depending on whether *non inuenta* is regarded as equivalent to a temporal clause, or to the protasis of a conditional sentence. The difference is very slight: either 'when you were lost you were a lighter grief than now that you have been found'; or 'if you had not been found, you would have been a lighter grief than you are now in your discovery'.

For *eras=esses* cf. *Am.* 1, 6, 34: 'solus eram, si non saeuus adesset amor'; the usage is found in poetry and Silver Latin.

Note that the distinction once made between *inuenire* and *reperire* cannot be maintained, cf. *Ex P.* 3, 1, 34: 'inuenies, uere si reperire uoles'.

quodque unum potes: cf. 731: 'quos potuit solos . . .'   657
ad: 'in answer to'; cf. 503 n.

thalamos taedasque: of marriage; cf. Virg. *Aen.* 4, 18: 'si 658 non pertaesum thalami taedaeque fuisset'.

659 Compare what Daphne's father says to her in 481-2.

660 **uir**: for the lengthening of the short syllable at the rise of the foot cf. *Aen.* 4, 222: 'tum sic Mercurium adloquitur ac talia mandat'. See Postgate, *Prosodia Latina* p. 29 f.

662 **esse deum**: subject of *nocet*: cf. Cic. *Para.* 6, 51: 'non esse cupidum pecunia est; non esse emacem uectigal est'.

praeclusa . . .: the phrase is from Lucretius 5, 373: 'haut igitur leti praeclusa est ianua . . .' and Ovid uses a similar figure in *Tr.* 3, 2, 23-4: 'quo totiens nostri pulsata sepulcri / ianua, sed nullo tempore aperta fuit?'

663 Note the effective spondaic movement.

664 **talia**: adverbial accusative, 'in such fashion'; cf. 753 *omnia*. **maerentem** refers to Inachus.—**submouet**: 'pushes away', cf. 6, 274: 'populum submouerat aris' and 12, 231: 'submouet instantes raptamque furentibus aufert'.

stellatus: because of his many eyes (cf. 723 *stellantibus*). In the same way the newt was called *stellio* because of the starlike spots on its back. It is possible that there is a glance at the theory that identified Argus with the starry sky (see Roscher *Lexikon* vol. 1, p. 539).

665 **diuersa**: 'distant', cf. Cic. *Verr.* 3, 192: 'loca inter se maxime diuersa'.

666 **procul**: simply means 'at a distance', 'away', and does not necessarily imply that the distance is great; cf. 5, 114: 'quem procul adstantem . . . inridens', 4, 357: 'omni ueste procul iacta', 12, 359: 'sed procul a telo Theseus ueniente recessit', Virg. *Ecl.* 6, 16: 'serta procul tantum capiti delapsa iacebant' and Page's note.

668 **Phoronidos**: *Phoroneus*, like *Arestor* (624 n.), was an ancient Argive hero. He is said to be the son of Inachus, so Io will be his sister. O. uses the patronymic loosely as a fine-sounding name for Io.

ultra: cf. 530.

669 **natum**: i.e. Mercury. Lucian reports the conversation that ensued, in *Dialogues of the Gods* 3—pleasantly enough.

partu: to be taken with *enixast*, not *lucida*.

670 **Pleias**: Maia, one of the Pleiades or seven daughters of Atlas and Pleione; hence *lucida*.

det imperat: the *ut* is sometimes omitted in prose too, cf. Caes. *B.G.* 3, 11: 'huic mandat Remos reliquosque Belgas adeat atque in officio contineat', Livy 22, 49, 10: 'nuntia

publice patribus urbem Romanam muniant'. See Madvig 372
(b), Obs. 4.

> 'He wings his heeles, puts on his Felt, and takes 671
> His drowsie Rod; the Towre of Ioue forsakes; -4
> And, winding, stoops to Earth.'
>
> Sandys.

Compare Virgil's fine description in *Aen.* 4, 238 ff.—**alas:**
Mercury's winged sandals, or *talaria*, made of gold. **uirgam:**
the *caduceus*, an olive staff with two snakes twined round it
towards the top. **tegimen:** his *petasus*, a hat worn by travellers,
with a low crown and broad brim. As messenger of the gods
Mercury is equipped like a herald.

parua morast: contrast 214.

sumpsisse: cf. 176 n.; but here the perf. inf. emphasises the
speed of the action.

The description of how Mercury dressed and undressed has a
Homeric ring about it, cf. 398 n.

dum uenit abductas: 'stolen during the course of his journey'. *677
For *abducere* used of cattle-lifting cf. *Her.* 16, 357: 'abducta
armenta recepi', *Tr.* 3, 10, 65: 'quae nequeunt secum ferre aut
abducere, perdunt', Plin. *N.H.* 4, 120: 'cuius armenta Hercules
abduxerit'. Mercury was the god of thieves.

cantat: 'plays on', cf. *Tr.* 5, 10, 25: 'sub galea pastor iunctis
pice cantat auenis'; Pl. *Epid.* 500: 'ueni ut fidibus cantarem
seni'.

auenis=*fistula* (688), the instrument that we call the 'Pan-
pipe'.—'When shepherds pipe on oaten straws . . .' *Love's
Labour's Lost* 5, 2, 900.

structis: explained by 711-2. So O. talks of *structos uersus*,
because the words composing the lines are fitted compactly
together (*Ex P.* 2, 5, 19).

uoce: 'music'. The poets use the word of other sounds than *678
that of the human voice; cf. 338, and *Fasti* 6, 9: 'secretus ab
omni uoce locus'.

noua: explained by 687-8.

poteras: a polite invitation, almost equivalent to 'Why don't 679
you . . ' cf. Virg. *Ecl.* 1, 79: 'hic tamen hanc mecum poteras
requiescere noctem'. Grammatically it can be explained as the
apodosis of a suppressed condition: 'If you liked, you could . . .'
see 621 n.

Golding's version is worth transcribing:

'Good fellow mine I praie thee hartilie
Come sit downe by me on this hill, for better foode I knowe
Thou shalt not find in all these feelds, and (as the thing doth
     showe)
It is a coole and shadowie plot, for shepheards verie fit'.

682   **Atlantiades:** see 670 n.—The repetitions in this passage—
viz. *multa loquendo . . . sermone, uincere . . . euincere, parte . . .
parte, reperta . . . reperta*—together with the rhyme of *loquendo
. . . canendo*, must be intentional. O. seems to be aiming at an
effect of drowsy monotony, for Mercury was trying to put
Argus to sleep. Sandys translates 687-8 thus:
'He asks who did invent
     (With that he yawn'd) that late-found instrument',
representing the repeated word by a yawn.

683   **detinuit:** 'occupied', cf. *Ex P.* 4, 10, 67: ' "detinui" dicam
"tempus curasque fefelli" ', and *Tr.* 5, 7, 39: 'detineo studiis
animum falloque dolores'.

685   The conflict of ictus and accent makes one feel the effort that
Argus made; cf. 294. The fact that O.'s hexameters are pre-
dominantly dactylic makes his use of consecutive spondees
doubly effective.

686   **quamuis:** frequently used by O. with the indicative, e.g. *Am.*
1, 15, 14: 'quamuis ingenio non ualet, arte ualet'.

688   **qua ratione:** a common prose phrase, e.g. Caes. *B.G.* 7, 37, 7:
'reliqua qua ratione agi placeat constituunt', Cic. *Lael.* 26:
'quid enim refert qua me ratione cogatis?', *Cluent.* 45: 'qua
ratione Habitum ueneno tollere conatus sit cognoscite'.

689   O. often employs the device of telling a story within a story.
One of the most extended examples occurs in Book 10, where the
lay that Orpheus sings in the Underworld contains the stories of
Hyacinthus, Pygmalion, Cinyras, and Adonis; in the course of
the last Venus tells Adonis the tale of Atalanta.

690   **Nonacrinas:** poetical for 'Arcadian'. *Nonacris* was a mountain
in northern Arcadia.

691   **una:** cf. 227 n.
     Syringa: σῦριγξ=L. *fistula:* συρίζω is related to *susurro.*
—This charming story resembles that of Apollo and Daphne in
idea, but O. tells it in quite a different way, as if to show how
similar material can be variously treated. If the earlier story
suggests the *Amores*, this is somewhat reminiscent of Virgil's
Eclogues. This pastoral atmosphere is wonderfully evoked by

Debussy's beautiful solo for unaccompanied flute, entitled
Syrinx.—Shelley has given the story an interpretation of his own
in the *Hymn of Pan*:

> 'And then I changed my pipings,—
> Singing how down the vale of Maenalus
>   I pursued a maiden and clasped a reed.
> Gods and men, we are all deluded thus!
>   It breaks in our bosom and then we bleed'.

non semel: = *saepe*. 692

Ortygiam . . . deam: Diana is called Ortygian because Ortygia 694
('Quail-island') was another name for Delos, her birth-place.

ipsaque . . .: 'and by her chastity too'. Cf. 476: 'innuptaeque
aemula Phoebes'.

ritu . . . Dianae: the dress of a huntress; there is a good picture 695
in Rich under *succinctus*.

Latonia: because *Latona* is the Latin form of Leto, mother of *696
Apollo and Diana.

corneus: prob. 'of horn', cf. 455 n. But in *Her.* 4, 83 697
'uenabula cornea' are 'hunting-spears of cornel-wood'.

foret: for *esset*, cf. 151 n.

sic quoque . . .: 'even so (i.e. in spite of her bow) she passed 698
for Diana'. Cf. 13, 896: 'sed sic quoque erat tamen Acis'.

acuta: so we talk of pine-*needles*. The word for the *cone* is 699
nux: A.A. 2, 424: 'quasque tulit folio pinus acuta nuces'.

Mercury breaks off because Argus has fallen asleep (713). O. 700
finishes the story for the reader's benefit. The device enables him
to introduce a little variety by using indirect speech.

restabat: in Ciceronian prose would require *ut* after it, cf.
685: 'pugnat euincere'. Livy has 'nec aliud restabat quam . . .
corrigere' (44, 4, 8).

fugisse: like the other infinitives, loosely dependent on 701
restabat; lit. 'it remained that the nymph fled . . .'

Ladonis: 'The river which drains the basin (of Pheneus) is 702
the Ladon, the most romantically beautiful of all the rivers of
Greece. Milton's fancy dwelt on "sanded Ladon's lilied banks",
—even the prosaic Pausanias exclaimed that there was no fairer
river either in Greece or in foreign lands (8, 25, 13); and among
the memories which I brought back from Greece I recall none
with more delight than those of the days I spent in tracing the
river from its birthplace in the lovely lake . . .' Frazer, *Folklore in
the O.T.* vol. 1, p. 164.

704 **se:** in a subordinate clause *se* and *suus* refer to the subject of the main clause when the subordinate clause expresses the thought or intention of that subject. See Madvig 490 (c).

706 **corpore pro nymphae:** for this order cf. 35: 'speciem in orbis'.

707 **suspirat:** one might have expected the subjunctive, but *dum* in poetry and Silver Latin often retains the present indicative in indirect speech; e.g. Cic. *Tusc.* 1, 101: 'dic, hospes, Spartae nos te hic uidisse iacentes / dum sanctis patriae legibus obsequimur'.

708 One can hear the rustling of the reeds, and there is a certain thinness about the vowels that suits 'the weak and plaintive sound'. Lucretius has a similar passage about the discovery of the Pan-pipe, 5, 1382-3: 'et zephyri, caua per calamorum, sibila primum / agrestes docuere cauas inflare cicutas', 'and the whistlings of the zephyr through hollow reeds . . .'

709 **arte noua . . . captum:** cf. 678: 'uoce noua captus'.

710
'Yet, O sweet (said he),
Together euer thus conuerse will we.'
Sandys.

712 **tenuisse:** the subject is still *deum* from 709.—*nomen* is the emphatic word in the line; he held, not Syrinx herself, but only her name.

713 **Cyllenius:** because Mt. Cyllene in Arcadia was Mercury's birthplace, cf. Virg. *Aen.* 4, 258: 'Cyllenia proles'.

714 **adoperta:** sc. *esse.*—*succubuisse* seems to be used absolutely. Elsewhere O. adds *somno*, e.g. *Her.* 12, 49: 'lumina custodis succumbere nescia somno'. Possibly here *somno* is to be taken with both verbs. *adoperta* as an adjective seems less good.

716 **medicata:** 'magic, charmed', cf. *Her.* 12, 107: 'flammea subduxi medicato lumina somno'. There may be a reminiscence of this passage in Stat. *Theb.* 2, 11: 'medica firmat uestigia uirga'.

717 **falcato . . . ense:** the *harpe*, a sword equipped near its point with a hook that projected backwards from the edge of the blade towards the hilt. It is also called *hamatus ensis* (5, 80) and cf. 4, 720: 'ferrum curuo tenus abdidit hamo.' Illustrated by Rich under *hamus* (3).

nutantem: cf. the description of Sleep in 11, 620: 'summaque percutiens nutanti pectora mento'.

718 **saxo:** 'from the rock', cf. 679.

719 **praeruptam . . . rupem:** Housman compared 386 'pauido . . . pauet'. One might perhaps add 83: 'finxit in effigiem'.

in tot lumina lumen: lit. 'the light you had for all those lights 720 of yours'. *in* is sometimes used in the sense of 'for', e.g. Cic. *Rab. Post.* 34: 'regem . . . scripsisse nullam pecuniam Gabinio nisi in rem militarem datam', 'except for military purposes'; Sen. *Contr.* 7, 18, 7:'incurrit quaestio an uenenum habere in mortem suam liceat'; Roby 1977.—For a longer example of such repeated words see 15, 88:

> heu quantum scelus est in uiscera uiscera condi
> congestoque auidum pinguescere corpore corpus
> alteriusque animantem animantis uiuere leto.

excipit: the literal meaning—'takes them out'; Cels. 7, 12, 1: 722 'forcipe dens excipiendus est'.

uolucrisque suae: the peacock, brought to the Mediterranean world from India and Ceylon.

exarsit: more usu. with an explanatory abl. such as *ira,* 724 *indignatione* etc., but for the absolute use cf. Cic. *De Or.* 1, 233: 'cuius responso sic iudices exarserunt', Livy 8, 4, 7: 'quis dubitat exarsisse eos'.

Erinyn: here a tormenting Demon; contrast 241.—Aeschylus 725 makes it the ghost of Argus that haunts Io (*P.V.* 568).

oculis animoque: for the pairing cf. 4, 129: 'iuuenemque oculis animoque requirit', 12, 529: 'pariterque animis oculisque secutus'. *Her.* 16, 101: 'te uigilans oculis, animo te nocte uidebam' might justify the interpretation that in our passage *oculis* refers to the daytime, *animo* to the night; Io was allowed no respite.

stimulos: cf. *P.V.* 598 κέντροις φοιταλέοισιν. 726
exercuit: 'drove her on'. *727

Io still had to reach the Nile before she could bring the long 728 tale of her sufferings to an end. For *restabas* with the dat. in this sense cf. 2, 655: 'restabat fatis aliquid'—Ocyroe has been prophesying to Chiron and has told him part of his fate, but part still remains to be told.

labori: =*laboribus,* 'hardships, sufferings'; Cic. *Fin.* 2, 105: 'suauis laborum est praeteritorum memoria'—a translation of a line from Eur. *Andromeda* (Nauck² Fr. 133): ἀλλ' ἡδύ τοι σωθέντα μεμνῆσθαι πόνων.

positisque: it seems best to regard the main clause as beginning 729 here, though it is possible to hold that it does not begin until 734.

ardua: 'looking upwards'. The word is used of a rearing 730 horse in Virg. *Aen.* 11, 638: 'quo sonipes ictu furit arduus'; of

Entellus raising himself to his full height in *Aen.* 5, 479: 'librauit dextra media inter cornua caestus / arduus, effractoque illisit in ossa cerebro'.—L. and S. take the word with *sidera* in the next line (cf. *arduus aether* 151), but this seems less likely.

731   For the thought cf. 3, 241: 'circumfert tacitos tamquam sua bracchia uultus', and the striking picture of Cassandra in *Aen.* 2, 405-6: 'ad caelum tendens ardentia lumina frustra, / lumina, nam teneras arcebant uincula palmas'.

    tollens . . . uultus: O. may intend this as a hint that Io is soon to be turned back into human shape, for 'erectos ad sidera tollere uoltus' (86) is the distinguishing mark of humanity.

732   **luctisono:** a ἅπαξ λεγόμενον; it has an archaic tinge and may be a reminiscence. For similar compounds cf. *ueliuolus, fluctifragus, altitonans.* Quintilian (1, 5, 65 ff.) in discussing *compositae uoces* quotes from Pacuvius the line: 'Nerei repandirostrum incuruiceruicum pecus'. His final judgement on the question of whether such words are suited to Latin is this: 'res tota magis Graecos decet, nobis minus succedit'.

733   **queri cum:** the regular phrase for 'to complain to' someone; 10, 724: 'questaque cum fatis', *Tr.* 3, 8, 39: 'querar ut cum Caesaris ira' (=cum irato Caesare), Cic. *Fam.* 3, 10, 7: 'quererer tecum atque expostularem'.

735   **tandem:** best taken in the *ut* clause.

    'in' que: cf. 456 n.

737   **haec:** there is prob. a double meaning; either 'this sort of behaviour on my part will never again cause you pain', or 'Io will never etc.'—implying that there may be others. Jove intends Juno to take the promise in the first sense; he swears to it only in the second.

738-9 **uultus . . . fuit:** the second clause is simply a variation of the first; cf. 724.

    illa: this pronoun marks a change of subject, as often; cf. 503, 543, 611, 646, 685.

    fugiunt: 'fall away', cf. Sen. *H.F.* 994: 'medio spiculum collo fugit uolnere relicto', Hom. *Od.* 10, 393 τῶν δ' ἐκ μὲν μελέων τρίχες ἔρρεον.

741   **rictus:** usu. but not always of the wide mouth of animals. In *A.A.* 3, 283-4 advice is given on how to laugh: 'sint modici rictus paruaeque utrimque lacunae / et summos dentes ima labella tegant'.

742   **dilapsa:** of things dispersing, or dissolving; cf. Livy 41, 2:

'nebula matutina dilabente', Virg. *Georg.* 4, 410: 'aut in aquas tenues dilapsus abibit'.

absumitur: 'vanishes'; cf. Plin. *N.H.* 2, 184: 'bis anno absumi umbras'.

nymphe: a form often used by O., see 3, 345, 357; 4, 277; 8, 605; 9, 89 etc. [744]

officioque pedum: cf. Ter. *Eun.* 729: 'postquam surrexi, neque pes neque mens satis suom officium facit'.

erigitur: middle use of the passive as in 570, 538; cf. 9, 518: 'in latus erigitur'. Prose authors prefer *se* and the active, e.g. Cic. *Rosc. Am.* 60: 'statim homo se erexit', Caes *B.G.* 6, 27, 2: 'neque erigere sese aut subleuare possunt'. [745]

A delightful touch.—*uerba intermissa:* 'words for so long unused'; cf. Cic. *Tusc.* 1, 1: 'studia ... longo interuallo intermissa reuocaui'. [746]

dea: Io was identified with the Egyptian goddess Isis, because she too was represented as having the horns of a cow; cf. Her. 2, 41.—**linigera:** the priests of Isis wore linen and shaved their heads and bodies for the sake of ritual purity. They regarded wool as a sort of waste matter and therefore unclean; cf. Apul. *Apol.* 56: 'lana segnissimi corporis excrementum'. [747]

The ablative *turba* is best taken with *celeberrima;* cf. 6, 165: 'uenit comitum Niobe celeberrima turba', *Fasti* 4, 391: 'circus erit pompa celeber'.—'Now, fêted by a crowd of linen-clad priests, she is worshipped as a goddess'.

huic: dative of the agent; *gigno* can be used of father or mother.—The order is: 'Epaphus creditur esse tandem genitus huic de semine magni Iouis'. *tandem* because of Io's long sufferings. [*748]

Epaphus: Io's son was identified with the Egyptian Apis, the bull-god of Memphis; see Her. 3, 27.

iuncta parenti: 'next to those of his mother'. For the usual brachylogy cf. 115 n.; for *iuncta=contermina* cf. *Fasti* 1, 258: 'iuncta foris templa duobus'. [749]

Isis shared the sites of her temples with Sarapis, a god uniting in himself the characteristics of Osiris and Apis. The worship of Isis spread throughout the Mediterranean world in the Hellenistic Age along the main trade routes; eventually she became one of the most important divinities in the Pantheon. Her cult had a wide popular appeal because of its emotionalism, its elaborate and colourful ritual and its professional priesthood. She promised immortality to those initiated into her mysteries. See H. S. Jones, *Companion to Roman History* pp. 296 ff.

750 **animis . . . annis:** 'his match in heart and yeeres', Golding.— Ovid likes to play on these two words, e.g. 7, 658: 'pares annis animisque', 13, 550: 'non oblita animorum, annorum oblita suorum'. For similar turns cf. 2, 634: 'mixtoque oneri gaudebat honore', Lucr. 1, 901: 'non est lignis tamen insitus ignis', Cic. *Tusc.* 3, 64: 'nec uerbis solum, sed etiam uerberibus . . . plorare cogunt (pueros)'.

751 **Phaethon:** Ovid ends Book 1 with the first scene in the story of Phaethon, which is to be concluded in Book 2. Aeschylus had dramatised the tale in his lost *Heliades*—a title taken from the name of Phaethon's sisters—and some fragments survive of the *Phaethon* of Euripides. The quarrel here introduced between Epaphus and Phaethon is probably Ovid's own invention, so that he may have a satisfactory connexion between the story of Io and its successor.—In Plato's *Timaeus* 22 D, the Egyptian priest who talks to Solon intreprets Phaethon's disaster as a legendary account of a world conflagration: 'in fact' he says 'there is a declination of the heavenly bodies in their course round the earth . . . and at long intervals of time the surface of the earth is destroyed in a great fire'. Very much later the author of the treatise *De Astrologia*, falsely ascribed to Lucian, explains that Phaethon was really an astronomer who tried to plot out the sun's course through the sky, but died before he had completed his task. Some modern scholars believe that Phaethon's fall is a poetic representation of the sunset and of the fiery blaze in the western sky that often accompanies it.—The figure of Phaethon seems to have caught Shakespeare's imagination. There are several references to him in the plays, e.g.:

> Down, down I come; like glistering Phaethon
> Wanting the manage of unruly jades.
> *Richard II*, 3, **3.**

> Why, Phaethon,—for thou art Merops' son—
> Wilt thou aspire to guide the heavenly car,
> And with thy daring folly burn the world?
> Wilt thou reach stars because they shine on thee?
> *Two Gentlemen*, 3, 1.

752 **nec sibi cedentem:** i.e. not admitting his superiority, not giving precedence to him; cf. Cic. *Off.* 1, 149: 'cedere iis qui magistratum habebunt (debemus)'.

omnia: adverbial accusative 'in everything'. Golding has a 753
vigorous paraphrase:
> For euerie fond and trifling tale the which thy mother makes
> Thy giddie wit and harebraind head foorthwith for gospell
> takes.

imagine: 'idea'; of any vivid mental picture, e.g. Virg. *Aen.* 754
2, 560: 'subiit cari genitoris imago'.

tulit ad . . . matrem: a very human touch.—Jacobus Pontanus, 756
(a 17th-century editor) remarks: 'more puerorum . . . qui offensi
ab aequalibus rem ad parentes deferunt et ab iis auxilium ac
vindictam petunt'.

ille ego: cf. *Am.* 3, 8, 23: 'ille ego Musarum purus Phoebique 757
sacerdos'; occasionally too in prose, e.g. Cic. *Phil.* 7, 7: 'ego ille
qui semper pacis auctor fui'.

liber: 'outspoken, independent', cf. Hor. *Ep.* 1, 18, 1: 'liberrime
Lolli'.

ferox: 'quick-tempered'; cf. Cic. *Sen.* 33: 'infirmitas puerorum 758
et ferocitas iuuenum et grauitas iam constantis aetatis'.

nobi : for the phrase *opprobria dicere alicui* cf. Tib. 1, 3, 31:
'tibi dicere laudes', Pl. *Bacch.* 267: 'quotque innocenti ei dixit
contumelias'.

A great utterance, with more than one level of meaning when 760
taken out of its context.   -1

adsere: see 462 n. Seneca uses the expression: 'sera et
nepotibus demum nostris dies nota sit qua illum gens sua
caelo adserat' *(Dial.* 11, 12, 5).

Meropis: Merops, king of Ethiopia, was Clymene's husband. 763

perque suum . . . : in adjurations appeal is made to that which
is dearest to the heart of the person addressed. So Phaethon
begs Clymene, as she values the life of himself and of her
husband, and as she hopes for the happy marriage of his sisters,
to give him some token of his true parentage.—Cf. *Her.* 3, 107:
'perque tuum nostrumque caput'.

traderet orauit: see 670 n.   764

The order is: *Clymene (ambiguum* est utrum *magis mota* sit 765
precibus Phaethontis an ira criminis dicti sibi) porrexit etc. For
the omission of *utrum* cf. 578 n. *sit* is rarely omitted even in
verse and very seldom in prose: Cic. *Off.* 1, 152: 'potest incidere
saepe contentio . . . de duobus honestis utrum honestius .—
dicti sibi criminis: 'the accusation made against her'; for the 766
construction cf. Livy 45, 37, 6: 'cui nullum crimen, nullum

probrum dicere poterat, eius obtrectare laudes uoluit'.—caelo: poetical for *ad caelum*:—Virg. *Aen.* 5, 451: 'it clamor caelo'.

768   **coruscis:** 'flashing'. Henry (*Aeneidea* 1, pp. 462 f.) makes it clear that the word expresses alternate appearance and disappearance. So O. says of serpents in 4, 494: 'linguisque coruscant'. Virgil (*Aen.* 1, 164) applies the word to *siluae*, to describe how the wind catches the leaves and exposes every now and again their brighter under-side.

769   **auditque uidetque:** a fine panegyric of the sun is to be found in Plin. *N.H.* 2, 13. He writes: ˙hunc esse mundi totius animum ac planius mentem, hunc principale naturae regimen ac numen credere decet opera eius aestimantes. hic lucem rebus ministrat aufertque tenebras, hic reliqua sidera occultat inlustrat, hic uices temporum annumque semper renascentem ex usu naturae temperat, hic caeli tristitiam discutit atque etiam humani nubila animi serenat, hic suum lumen ceteris quoque sideribus faenerat, praeclarus, eximius, omnia intuens, omnia etiam exaudiens, ut principi litterarum Homero placuisse in uno eo uideo'. Homer's words in *Il.* 3, 277 are these: Ἠέλιός θ' ὅς πάντ' ἐφορᾷς καὶ πάντ' ἐπακούεις.

770   **temperat:** 'orders', 'controls'; cf. Plin. *loc. cit.*; *Met.* 4,169: 'siderea qui temperat omnia luce'; *F.* 4, 91 (of Venus): 'illa quidem totum dignissima temperat orbem'.

*771   **neget . . . uidendum:** the verb is equivalent to *ne det* and the gerundive like that in 624. '*sitque . . . nostris*' is a variation of *neget . . . mihi.*

773   A fine line, to which Christianity has added its own depth of meaning (cf. 760-1).

774   **contermina:** this adj. first appears in O.—Homer (*Od.* 1, 23) calls the Ethiopians, or 'Burnt-faces', ἔσχατοι ἀνδρῶν and says that they dwell in two groups, 'some where Hyperion sets, the others where he rises'. Herodotus (7, 70) agrees with the division, but places the first group above Egypt. When O. brought Epaphus into the story he was thinking of the Ethiopians near Egypt; now he is thinking of those that live near the rising sun.

775   **fert:** cf. 1 n.—**scitabere:** the second person of the future is often used for the imperative, e.g. Cic. *Fam.* 14, 8: 'facies ut sciam', 'let me know'.

776   **emicat:** 'dashes out'; cf. Virg. *Aen.* 6, 5: 'iuuenum manus emicat ardens / litus in Hesperium'.

concipit aethera mente: i.e. already the sky was his in imagina- 777
tion. For *mente concipere*='imagine' cf. 2, 76-7: 'forsitan et
lucos illic urbesque deorum / concipias animo'.—Dryden
translates: 'He longs the World beneath him to survey.'

sidereis: cf. 424 n.   779

transit: for the meaning 'pass *through*' cf. Cic. *Att.* 9, 3, 1:
'Domitii filius transiit Formias'.

ortus: when speaking of sunrise in the accusative O. always
uses the plural; see the interesting line 14, 386: 'tum bis ad
occasum, bis se conuertit ad ortus'. In the ablative the singular
is always used.

CRITICAL NOTES

Although we possess many MSS. of the *Metamorphoses*, the earliest of them, the Berne fragment, is no older than the 9th century, whereas several Virgilian MSS. date back to the 4th century. To determine the mutual relations of these numerous and late MSS. presents a problem of great complexity. The reader interested in a full discussion of the tradition is referred to Magnus's *Praefatio*, Slater's *Prolegomena*, and R. T. Bruère's 'The MS. Tradition of Ovid's Metamorphoses' (*Harvard Studies in Classical Philology*, vol. 50, 1939, pp. 95-122), where other important references will be found. Suffice it to say here that the extant MSS. fall into two classes: those that contain the *Narrationes* ascribed to a certain Lactantius or Luctatius, and those that have no trace of them. These *Narrationes* are prose paraphrases of the transformation stories and would appear to have formed part of a quite elaborately annotated edition of the *Metamorphoses* produced by some scholar of perhaps the 6th century. The class of MSS. which contain them, or traces of them, is known as O and is regarded as of greater authority than the second class, X. Of the MSS. listed below, ε M N and U belong to class O, the remainder, with the exception of α, whose derivation is disputed, to class X. The best representatives of O, that is M and N, finish just before the end of Book 14, so that the text of Book 15 is based on class X and its main representative, F.

The readings that follow are cited from the critical apparatuses of Magnus and Slater. Where the two are at variance, Slater is preferred.

α=fragmentum Bernense 363, 9th cent. containing 1, 1-199, 304-9, 773-9; 2, 1-22; 3, 1-56.

ε=fragmentum Harleianum 2610, 10th or 11th cent., containing 1-3, 622.

M=Marcianus Florentinus 225, 11th cent., ending at 14, 830.

F=Marcianus Florentinus 223, 11th or 12th cent.

L=Laurentianus Florentinus xxxvi 12, 11th or 12th cent., ending at 12, 298.

U=Urbinas Vaticanus 341, 11th or 12th cent.

E=Palatinus Vaticanus 1669, 12th cent.

N=Neapolitanus IV F 3, 12th cent.; the first hand ends at 14, 838.

h=Hauniensis 2008, 13th cent.

Plan.=a Greek prose translation by the 13th-cent. Byzantine monk, Maximus Planudes.

Magnus reads with the MSS. *qui quanto est pondere terrae,* 52-3 *pondere aquae leuior.* The reading in the text was found, according to Constantius Fanensis, by his friend Alexander Philumenos in an ancient MS.—*in peruetusto codice.* The passage has been fully discussed by Housman in his *Lucan* pp. xxvii ff. He rejects Magnus' reading not so much because of the clumsy anaphora as because its sense is faulty. He argues (i) that the reading implies that earth and water have the same weight; (ii) that it is plainly untrue to say that in weight air stands half-way between ether on the one hand and earth or water on the other.

massa latuere sub illa M Magnus, *fuerant caligine caeca* α, 70 *fuerant caligine multa* N. It is conceivable that the variant reading derives from Ovid's own hand, but more likely that it arose from a gloss on *massa*.

Magnus reads *erant* with α. But the singular is correct be- 99 cause, as Housman pointed out, *non* is not a conjunction. He compared Tib. 1, 10, 9: 'non arces, non uallus erat'. See too C. F. W. Mueller on Cic. *Off.* 1, 128: 'uultus oculi manuum motus teneat illud decorum'.

Magnus prefers α's *exsultauere* as being more vigorous (*Jahrb.* 134 *f. klass. Phil.* 1891 p. 700), but *insultauere* has much better authority and more point (see note).

subiecto ε M¹ N, *subiectae* α Magnus, *subiectum* L, *subiecto* 155 *Pelio Ossam* (cf. Virg. *G.* 1, 281) Heinsius. But names of mountains feminine in form are found, though very rarely, with masculine adjectives, e.g. 9, 165: 'nemorosum Oeten,' 204: 'altum Oeten' (M's reading in both places). The change of gender may have been made easier by the fact that all names of mountains with *mons* in apposition are masculine, e.g. Caes. *B.G.* 1, 2, 3: 'monte Iura altissimo' (see Neue *Formenlehre* vol. 1, p. 954, and Kuehner-Holzweissig, p. 261 A. 2).

temptanda ε M N², *temptata* α L Magnus. The former is 190 preferable. Jupiter, having sworn to destroy the human race, supports his decision by a general maxim or *sententia*. 'Granted', he says in effect, 'that it is desirable to try every expedient first, yet when a growth is clearly incurable (as this is) there is nothing for it but surgery'. The objections to *temptata* are (i) that every expedient has *not* been tried; Jupiter has simply heard rumours of human wickedness and made a reconnaissance; (ii) that the force of *sed* after it is not so good.

202 **tantae subito** ε L Plan. Burman, *tanto subitae* M U Magnus. The former seems to me slightly preferable.

218 **Arcados** ε Heinsius, *Archadis* M, *Archadas* N², *Archades* L. The first best explains the variants. Ovid is fond of Greek forms. Magnus prints *Arcadis*.

hic ε M Magnus. *hic* makes no sense unless understood temporally, which is awkward here. *hinc* 'after that' is common in such descriptions of journeys, e.g. Hor. *Sat.* 1, 5, 50: 'hinc nos Coccei recipit plenissima uilla', *ib.* 47 and 86.

225 **comparat** U, *comprimere* ε, *me parat* (*me* in erasure) M Magnus. For the corruption of *comparat* Housman compared *Tr.* 2, 267-8: 'si quis tamen urere tecta / comparat', where some MSS. give *coeperit*, others *apparat* etc. The word is well suited to criminal attempts, cf. *F.* 2, 780: 'comparat indigno uimque dolumque toro'.

235 **uertitur** ε L U Heinsius, *utitur* M Magnus. The second is less vivid and may have arisen from a misreading of the abbreviated form *ūtitur* (=*uertitur*).

239 **lurent** Housman (*Trans. of the Cambridge Philological Soc.* 3, p. 140), *lucent* MSS. Magnus. Housman regards *lucent* as inadequate. The adj. *luridus* is common, the noun *luror* very rare and the verb *lureo* not in the dictionaries, but, he points out, it has been preserved once in the *Metamorphoses:* in 2, 776, where the MSS. have *liuent*, Robinson Ellis found the reading *lurent* in a Bodleian codex of excerpts. Cf. 4, 715.

258 **moles operosa** E L U Lactantius *De Ira Dei* 23, 6, Heinsius, *moles obsessa* h Magnus, *proles obsessa* ε M N Ehwald. *mundi proles* is an unusual expression which Ehwald takes to mean 'everything that lives in the world', but no parallel is adduced.—The choice between *obsessa* and *operosa* is more difficult. I prefer the latter because it contributes more to the total meaning of the sentence; *obsessa* is really implied already by the combination of *correpta* (257) and *laboret*.

273 **labor perit** E L Heinsius, *perit labor* cett. Magnus. The former produces a better pattern of words, and since it is a little less obvious was more likely to have suffered alteration.

292 *erant* M Magnus. In support of the singular Housman quoted

Virg. *E.* 8, 58: 'omnia uel medium fiat mare', *Dirae* 46: 'cinis omnia fiat'; add *Met.* 15, 529: 'unumque erat omnia uulnus'. For a brief discussion of such attraction of the number of the verb to that of the predicate see Loefstedt *Syntactica* 2 (1933), 118-9.

Parnasos ε E, *Parnasus* cett. Magnus. It is more likely that the 317 rarer Greek form is right, cf. 218.

tum F Heinsius, *tunc* ε M N Magnus. *tunc* before a guttural 339 is hardly ever found in the best MSS. of Virgil, and therefore is unlikely to be right in Ovid; see Housman's *Juvenal*, p. xxi, footnote.

sola Housman (*Trans. of the Cambridge Phil. Soc.* 3, p. 141), 345 *loca* MSS. Magnus. Housman maintains that *loca* cannot mean dry land as opposed to water, and quotes *Her.* 7, 57-8: 'nec uiolasse fidem temptantibus aequora prodest: perfidiae poenas exigit ille locus' and other passages to support the assertion. The proper contrast, he says, is *sola*; cf. Cat. 63, 40: 'sola dura, mare ferum'. For the origin of the corruption he compares Virg. *G.* 2, 512, where P has *lose* for *sole.*—Slater notes that Heinsius had already suggested *sola* in an unpublished annotation, but he himself prefers *iuga*, if *loca* is to be changed at all.

caecisque ε h, *cetisque* L, *caecis* cett. Magnus. No other editor 388 appears to have printed ε's *-que* (indeed Slater does not think it worth recording), but it is the more difficult reading, and further, *repetere* is not used with *secum, mecum* etc. elsewhere in Ovid. For this type of ἀπὸ κοινοῦ construction cf. *Tr.* 3, 8, 35-6: 'haeret et ante oculos ueluti spectabile corpus / astat fortunae forma legenda meae'.

datae sortis E F N² Plan. Heinsius, *deae sortis* ε N¹, *deae* 389 *sortes* M. Magnus punctuates *uerba deae, sortis.* Slater would prefer *uerba, deae sortis:* for the phrase he compares 10, 567: 'territa sorte dei'. But the disadvantages of reading *deae sortis,* in spite of its better authority, are two: (i) *latebris* must then = *ambagibus,* a meaning for which no parallel has been adduced, for such places as Cic. *De Div.* 2, 111: 'adhibuit latebram obscuritatis' and *Fam.* 3, 12: 'nullam ne in tabellae quidem latebra fuisse absconditam maleuolentiam' are not on a par with our passage; (ii) the ambiguity about the correct punctuation (though see 115 n.) and indeed this particular use of apposition are not true to Ovid's manner. As against this it might perhaps be argued that Ovid is wittily trying to reproduce in his reader the sense of obscurity experienced by Deucalion and Pyrrha! However, *datae* meets both difficulties: *latebris* has its normal meaning and *datae* picking up *dedit* (381) is thoroughly Ovidian.

426   The MSS. and editors read:
-7   'et in his quaedam modo coepta per ipsum
              nascendi spatium, quaedam imperfecta suisque
              trunca uident numeris . . .'
but the contrast between *modo coepta* and *imperfecta* is poor.— Two parallel passages on the same subject, viz. spontaneous generation in Egypt, are relevant: (i) Pomponius Mela 1, 9, 52: 'per umentes campos quaedam nondum perfecta animalia sed tum primum accipientia spiritum et ex parte iam formata, ex parte adhuc terrena, uisuntur'; (ii) Diodorus 1, 10: φασὶ συνίστασθαι ζῷα, τινὰ μὲν εἰς τέλος ἀπηρτισμένα, τινὰ δὲ ἡμιτελῆ καὶ πρὸς αὐτῇ συμφυῆ τῇ γῇ. Paul. von Winterfeld, in *Hermes* 33, p. 169, arguing from the first of these, proposed that in our passage *modo coepta* and *imperfecta* should be transposed, and Slater approves. But Mela is describing only one class of animals, whereas Ovid is dealing with two (*quaedam . . . quaedam*), and von Winterfeld's transposition still leaves a poor contrast between them. The reading in the text was suggested by van Leeuwen (see Hartman, *De Ovidio Poeta* p. 90) and then (independently?) by Vollgraff (*Nikander-und Ovid* p. 101 ff.). It is based on the contrast between the two classes of complete and incomplete animals found in Diodorus.—Perhaps the scribe's eye passed from the *-ta* of *perfecta* to that of *coepta*, and he wrote 'et in his quaedam perfecta suisque . . .' The words omitted (viz. 'per ipsum nascendi spatium quaedam modo coepta') were then supplied elsewhere on the page. This caused confusion; *perfecta* was altered to *imperfecta* to make it harmonise with its surroundings, and *quaedam modo coepta* was wrongly placed before *per ipsum...spatium*. For such omission of a line caused by homoeoteleuton of two letters cf. 304-5, where ε M N read:
              'nat lupus inter oues nec uires fulminis apro
              crura nec ablato prosunt uelocia ceruo'.

441   **numquam letalibus** Housman (*loc. cit.*), *et numquam talibus* MSS. Magnus, *non umquam talibus* Heyne, *sed numquam talibus* Polle. The *et* of the MSS. is awkward because *deus arquitenens* forms a single idea, viz. Apollo. Housman imagines the stages

in the corruption to have been (i) *te talibus*, (ii) *te* becoming *et*, (iii) *et* transposed *metri gratia*.

de domitae N Heinsius. *perdomitae* cett. Magnus. The first is 447 perhaps a little more difficult, and Ovid almost always uses a preposition in such expressions, cf. 5, 411; 6, 71; 8, 235; 13, 648 etc. However, 14, 348 is an exception: 'nomine dicta suo Circaea reliquerat arua'. Perhaps *perdomitae* arose as a correction of the misreading *dedomitae*, which looks, but in fact is not, a possible Latin word.

I have printed the text as Magnus gives it. To set forth in full 544 the MS. readings of this vexed passage would require too much ff. space for an appendix such as this. It is enough to say that the MSS. offer various confusions of the following two versions:

    (i) uicta labore fugae spectans Peneidas undas,
       'fer, pater', inquit, 'opem si flumina numen habetis;
       qua nimium placui, mutando perde figuram.'
    (ii) uicta labore fugae 'Tellus', ait, 'hisce uel istam
       quae facit ut laedar, mutando perde figuram.'

Magnus holds that the second version is an interpolation introduced at a later date than the Argumenta of Lactantius to bring Ovid's version of the story into line with the current account of Daphne's transformation. E. K. Rand (*Class. Phil.* 1916, p. 49) assigns both versions to Ovid's original text and considers that such extensive repetition is quite in his manner, comparing 1, 361-2, 481-2; 6, 281-2; 8, 285-6, 697-8. Others, such as R. Helm, see in this passage evidence of a revision of the *Metamorphoses* on the part of Ovid himself.

Peneos Probus on *Georg.* 4, 317, *Peneus* MSS. Magnus. There are 569 two other places where this proper name occurs in the nominative in the *Metamorphoses*; *Peneos* is given in the first (2, 243) by ε F and in the second (7, 230) by N U¹. In both places Magnus prints the Greek form.

Apidanus Politian Heinsius, *Eridanus* MSS. Magnus. Heinsius 580 reports that he found the intermediate form *Epidanus* in some MSS. *Eridanus* will not do here, because a local Thessalian river is needed. For the confusion cf. Luc. *De Bello Civ.* 6, 373: 'Apidanos (*Eridanus* dett.) numquamque celer nisi mixtus Enipeus'. In *Met.* 7, 228 the MSS. give *Eridani* while Plan. has ’Απιδανοῦ. I have here adopted the Gk. termination, cf. *Sperchios, Amphrysos*.

in Argos Lucian Mueller. *in agros* MSS. Magnus. *medios in* 601 *agros* seems too vague, whereas *medios* ... *Argos* = μέσον Ἄργος of *Odyssey* 1, 344; 4, 726 etc, as R. J. Getty has pointed out to me. For the confusion cf. *F.* 5, 651: 'magnaque pars horum desertis uenerat Argis', which is Heinsius' certain correction of MSS. *agris*; see also *Met.* 14, 476; 15, 164.

637   **conatoque** E U Heinsius, *conataque* ε. *et conata* M N Magnus. There is the same choice in *Her.* 14, 91, where Palmer prints *conatoque* on the supposition that *que* may well have fallen out before *queri*. Or perhaps the misreading *conataque* gave rise to *et conata.*

652   **niuea** R. J. Getty, *niuae* ε, *n(iueae* in erasure by the second hand) h, *niueae* cett. edd. It is not in accordance with Ovid's practice to have two such adjectives as *gementis* and *niueae* attached to one noun. ε's reading would seem to point to an original *niuea* with the last two letters interchanged, for ε often writes *ae* as *e*. For the phrase cf. 10, 272: 'conciderant ictae niuea ceruice iuuencae' (where Magnus misprints *icta*).

677   **abductas** Mureti Excerpta, Heinsius, *adductas* MSS. Magnus. Ehwald takes *hac* with *adductas*, i.e. the goats were drawn towards Mercury by his magic wand; but *hac* goes more naturally with *agit*. Otherwise 'dum uenit adductas' is usually translated 'collected as he went', but does *adducere* ever mean to 'collect'? *abductas* gives much better sense (see notes). For the confusion see *Tr.* 3, 10, 65, where *adducere* is wrongly given for *abducere* by EHKVβ and π.

678   **uoce noua captus custos Iunonius** *arte* ε M N, *Iunonis et arte* h, *uoce nouae ... artis (ar tis* E) E L U Plan. *uoce noua et captus ... arte* Ehwald Magnus. The reading in the text was taken by Burman from a MS. belonging to Jacques Auguste de Thou. For the form of the expression cf. *R.A.* 371: ˙at tu quicumque es,' *Tr.* 3, 3, 75: 'at tibi qui transis ne sit graue quisquis amasti'. *arte* may possibly have come in from 709.

696   **falleret** *ut* M Magnus. But *et* may well have fallen out after the last syllable of *falleret* and *ut* have been inserted to fill the gap.

727   **exercuit** Postgate, *exterruit* codex Holkhamicus (15th cent.), *circuit* ε N¹, *terruit* M Magnus, ἐξεφόβησε Plan. Postgate's conjecture accounts for the variants and gives excellent sense; cf. Virg. *G.* 4, 453: 'non te nullius exercent numinis irae', *A.* 7, 378-80: 'turbo / quem pueri magno in gyro uacua atria circum˒ ... exercent'. Slater notes that Aeschylus makes Io

say (*P.V.* 585): ἄδην με πολύπλανοι πλάναι γεγυμνάκασιν, and cf. 592: γυμνάζεται.

huic Burney MS. 234 (13th cent.) Heinsius, *hinc* N U, *nc̄* F, **748** *nunc* ε M h Magnus. *nunc* is awkward because, whereas the *nunc* of 747 most naturally refers to Ovid's own time (so too 749-50: 'perque urbes . . . tenet'), it would in 748 refer to the past. Nor can it be taken with *creditur* in an attempt to overcome this difficulty, for Epaphus was believed to be the son of Jupiter long before Ovid's time.

fero ε, *loquor* cett. Magnus. ε jumps from *ficta* to *neget*, and **771** above the line has *fero*, which Robinson Ellis approves. Magnus holds that *fero* has come in from Virg. *A.* 2, 161: 'si uera feram', but this does not sound very convincing. It is more probable that the vulgate *loquor* is a gloss.

INDEX

TO THE EXPLANATORY NOTES